MW01493373

ALABAMA FOOTPRINTS Exploration

A Collection of
Lost & Forgotten Stories

Additional Alabama Footprints can be found on the websites:

www.alabamapioneers.com

www.daysgoneby.me

Follow on Facebook at:

http://www.facebook.com/alabamapioneers

http://www.facebook.com/daysgonebyme

and

Twitter

http://twitter.com/alabamapioneers

ALABAMA FOOTPRINTS Exploration

A Collection of

Lost & Forgotten Stories

by

Donna R. Causey

DEDICATION

This book is dedicated to all
my friends and family in Alabama

INTRODUCTION

From the time of the discovery of America through the time of DeSoto's daring expedition, restless, resolute and adventurous men crossed oceans in pursuit of their destiny.

The beginning of the Sixteenth Century was noted for illustrious monarchs that held dominion in Europe. These were Henry VIII of England, Francis I of France, Charles V of Spain, Leo X, Pope of Rome, and Suleyman the Magnificent, Sultan of Turkey. Each of them possessed talents that might have rendered any age wherein they happened to flourish conspicuous.

The Feudal System was beginning to die and the Middle Ages were giving way to modern times. It is not strange that in such an age great enterprises were undertaken in the New World.

This book includes lost & forgotten stories of the explorations and settlement of the state of Alabama.

Table of Contents

Spanish Explorers

De Soto's Interpreter Was Almost Roasted By The Indians

Once Christopher Columbus discovered America, other explorers from many countries quickly followed in his path. One of these explorers was Pánfilo de Narváez.

Pánfilo de Narváez

Born in Spain, Pánfilo de Narváez first embarked to Jamaica in 1510 as a soldier and completed several other trips to the New World. On June 17, 1527, with a fleet of five ships and six hundred men, he arrived on the west coast of Florida in April 1528. His expedition was weakened by storms and desertions.

Narváez was forced to land with 300 men near the Rio de las Palmas—at what is currently known as the Jungle Prada Site in St. Petersburg, Florida among hostile natives, where he was soundly

3

defeated by the Indians.

Unable to find the gold and other riches he sought and tired of the hostilities with the Indians, Narváez ordered the construction of four rafts to return to the sea. Narváez party moved slowly westwards with some men on land and others on the raft. As the party was crossing a river the wind pulled the raft to sea, with Narváez on board, and he was never seen again. Of the original company, only four survived and eventually made their way to Mexico City eight years later to report the fate of Narváez.

Meanwhile, Spain had sent explorers in search of Narváez. Jean Ortiz, who would later become De Soto's interpreter in the wilds of Alabama, was a soldier on one of these ships. He arrived with other Spaniards in America and was almost roasted alive by the Indians for his effort.

The traditional story states that when Jean Ortiz arrived, the men on the ship were captured by the Indians. All their clothing was removed and the soldiers were compelled to run for their lives while the Indians shot at them with their deadly arrows. Ortiz alone survived.

"The Indians captured him and were about to roast him on a wooden gridiron, when his life was spared through the entreaties of a beautiful girl, a 'Southern Pocahontas', the daughter of Uceta the Indian Chief."

Instead of being burned alive, Ortiz was given a responsibility by the chief to take care of their temple situated on the edge of the dark, dense forest where the bodies of their dead were interred. The lids were kept upon boxes containing the dead by means of weights. Ortiz was ordered to protect the dead from the incursions of wild animals and death was to be the penalty if a solitary body was removed.

One night he grew weary and fell asleep, but luckily he was awakened by the falling of a coffin lid. Seizing his bow he rushed out, saw in the dim distance a clump of bushes, from whence proceeded a sound as of the crunching of bones. "He directed thither a swift arrow and soon all was still. Proceeding to the spot he found the dead body of a child, which he replaced in its box, and an enormous panther lying dead, which he dragged into the town." His efforts gained the respect of the Indians.

Three years later, a war broke out between the Uceta and a neighboring tribe. It was the custom among the Indians to make a sacrifice of a human life to appease the evil spirit which caused the war, and Jean Ortiz was selected as the victim. The daughter of the chief heard of the plan, and again saved Ortiz's life. In the dead of night, she led him a mile away to safety and told him to go to Mucoso, a chieftain whom she had promised to wed, for protection. The chieftain received him kindly and promised him that if any white man came to that country, Ortiz would be allowed to return to his people.

When De Soto arrived twelve years later, Ortiz was rescued when the army camped beside Tampa Bay. He became one of De Soto's soldiers and since he'd been a captive for many years, he was able to communicate with the Indians all along the coast. This made him very useful to De Soto as interpreter.

This story of Jean Ortiz is related by Historian, Albert J. Pickett's, in his book, *History of Alabama,* along with many other historical accounts of De Soto's travels in the Southeast. This account seems to have been derived mainly from a Portuguese narrative about De Soto's travels written long after his trip to America. General Thomas S. Woodward disputed many of the dramatic points of this narrative in a letter written to Albert J. Pickett in 1858.

Thomas Simpson Woodward was a Brigadier General in Georgia's militia in 1824 and he was an expert on the Creek Indians. In his letter addressed to Historian Albert J. Pickett on August 12, 1858, Woodward disagreed with the accuracy of the narrative on Jean Ortiz. His reasons were:

- Panthers do not feed on putrid flesh. They only feed on fresh kill.

5

- Burying the dead in raised boxes was an unknown Native American practice known to him and seemed improbable in "a country infested with animals such as wolves and other animals which preyed upon the dead."

In the letter, he also stated the following about the Portuguese narrative: "If a man willfully misrepresents one thing, he will another; and if he does it ignorantly once, he is liable to do it again."

Considering the time that has past, we will probably never know if this Portuguese narrative is true, but it is very interesting.

De Soto Was Refused Indian Maidens To Accompany Him

The main purpose of De Soto's expedition to America was to find gold. Gold was the great object of nearly all the Spanish explorers and conquerors at the time. They had successfully found it in Peru and De Soto hoped to find even more in the Americas.

Hernando DeSoto

His army was well-provided for with helmets, breastplates, shields, coats of steel armor, swords, lances, cross-bows, guns called arquebuses, and one cannon. The Spanish cavaliers numbered two hundred and thirteen and were said to have been "the most gallant and graceful men of all Spain."

7

Fleet greyhounds and large, fierce blood-hounds, with chains, handcuffs and collars for the neck, were used to aid in capturing and securing Indians whenever it might be needful. Workmen of various trades, with needful tools and large quantities of steel and iron, and scientific men with crucibles for refining gold, accompanied the expedition.

De Soto was also provided with a large drove of hogs, some cattle, and mules to travel with them into the wilderness. He had enough food to last two years and European merchandise for the purpose of trade. Twelve priests, eight other ecclesiastics, and four monks, with the needful robes of office, sacramental bread and wine, and various holy relics, made up the religious department of this exploring band.

Historian, Albert J. Pickett states: "Never was an expedition more complete, owing to the experience of De Soto, who upon the plains of Peru had ridden down hundreds in his powerful charges, and had poured out streams of savage blood with his broad and sweeping sword."

The following excerpt of their journey is from the Portuguese narrative about De Soto's trip and is probably very kind to De Soto.

> In early March, De Soto's band of soldiers left their winter quarters and traveled north and then turned to the northeast when they heard that gold could be found in that direction. They passed through what is now the State of Georgia and reached the area of Savannah and camped on the eastern bank of the river near an Indian town, later called Silver Bluff. In this town south of the present city of Augusta lived an Indian Queen, young, beautiful, an unmarried. She ruled the country around to a large extent.

> After De Soto's arrival, she glided across the river in a magnificent canoe, with many attendants, and after an interesting interview with De Soto, in which they exchanged presents, and passed many agreeable compliments, she invited him and his numerous followers over to her town.

The following day the expedition crossed the Savannah upon log rafts and in canoes. They quartered in the wigwams and under the spreading shades of the mulberry.

After remaining there for several weeks, De Soto left in May 1540, and took the beautiful young Queen with him. He resumed his march, passing up the Savannah to its head waters, and westward to the head waters of what is now called the Coosa. He then turned southward. and met with various adventures.

In early June 1540, De Soto traveled to a large Indian town where the town of Rome in the State of Georgia stands today. The chief of this town in his address of welcome to De Soto, and alluding to the latter's request to have corn collected sufficient to last his army two months, is reported to have said: "Here I have twenty barns full of the best which the country can afford." Besides corn, the Spaniards found, in this old Indian town, large quantities of bear's oil, laid up in gourds, walnut oil, equal to butter in its flavor, and pots of honey.

The Spaniards remained there for 30 days and shared the generous hospitality of these natives of Georgia.

When about to depart, De Soto, said, "of some of his unprincipled officers," demanded from this hospitable chief "a number of females to accompany them in their wanderings." The chief refused them this request. The Indian maidens of Georgia scorned to become the slaves and paramours of Spanish cavaliers.

In General T. S. Woodward's letter, he provides some of the Native American account of De Soto's trip through Alabama which differs slightly from the account above.

Indians say that none of DeSoto's men ever crossed to the east of the Oconee river, unless it was some of its head branches. A portion of the Spaniards made their way up the

9

Chattahoochee to Owe-Cowka, or the shoals of Columbus; there they called a halt, until they could correspond with the others that had gone farther east and north. Tallapoosa was then known as the river of towns; Tuckabatchee being the most important town in the nation, except Cusseta, was the point for the different commands to meet at.

A portion of them had traveled the route through northern Georgia, as you describe, and then a south-westerly course, through a portion of Alabama, reaching the Tallassees who then occupied a portion of what is now Talladega. Their principal town was on a creek that bears their name to this day, by the Indians.

In this time, the Spaniards had become obnoxious to the Indians; particularly those that had been quartered about where Columbus now is. This party left the Chattahoochee for Tuckabatchee and traveled pretty much the route that now leads from Columbus to Pole Cat Springs; their trail or trace passed through Tuskegee, and has been known as DeSoto's trace ever since.

I knew the country long before, and many that are now living knew it, as DeSoto's trace. The party that took this route missed their way, and instead of going to Tuckabatchee they reached the Tallapoosa lower down, where the Indians disputed their passage, and a fight ensued. The place they fought at took its name from the fight, Thlea Walla or Rolling Bullet; it is sometimes called Cuwally, and at others Hothleawally, by many, but Thlea Walla is the proper name.

The People Of Maubilla - Exterminated

De Soto entered the beautiful and fertile province of the Coosa River and experienced the hospitality of the generous natives.

Historian Albert Pickett statements below are based again on the words of the Portuguese narrative:

> The trail was lined with towns, villages, and hamlets, and many sown fields which reached from one to the other. The numerous barns were full of corn, while acres of that which was growing bent to the warm rays of the sun and rustled in the breeze. In the plains were plum trees peculiar to the country, and others resembling those of Spain. Wild fruit clambered to the tops of the loftiest trees, and lower branches were laden with delicious Isabella grapes.
>
> Far in the outskirts, De Soto was met by the Chief, seated upon a cushion, and riding in a chair supported upon the shoulders of four of his chief men. One thousand warriors, tall, active, sprightly, and admirably proportioned, with large plumes of various colors on their heads, followed him, marching in regular order. His dress consisted of a splendid mantle of martin skins, thrown gracefully over his shoulder, while his head was adorned with a diadem of brilliant feathers.
>
> Around him many Indians raised their voices in song, and others made music upon flutes. The steel clad warriors of Spain, with their glittering armour, scarcely equaled the magnificent display made by these natives of Alabama.
>
> After a speech of welcome by the Chief and a response by De Soto, they advanced together into the town, the former riding 'in his sedan chair,' the Spanish leader on his fiery war horse. This capital city contained five hundred houses, and here the adventurers remained twenty-five days, and again

marched southward.

Passing through Indian towns, gathering wild grapes which grew in great abundance, encamping at various places, De Soto arrived September 18, at a large town called Tallasee, surrounded by a wall and terraces. This town was on the Tallapoosa, along the banks of which river were extensive corn-fields, and Indian villages among these fields of ripening maize.

Again, General Woodward disagrees with some points in the above account. He states that:

The Tallassees or Tallaces, at that time evidently occupied a portion of Talladega; and from Talladega down to Thleawalla about suits the distance that they would have had to travel.

....The Tallasses never settled on the Tallapoosa river before 1756; they were moved to that place by James McQueen....Coosa and Tallase; those names are easy to pronounce; and they no doubt visited those towns; but you never hear Tuckabatchy named, for they were not at the place. It was at Thlea Walla that the Indians picked up those copper and brass plates that you have heard spoken of.

We return to the account from the Portuguese narrative:

While encamped at this place, (Tallasee) De Soto received an invitation from a renowned chief named Tuskaloosa to visit his capital city, a town called Maubila. De Soto accepted the invitation. He crossed the Tallapoosa, sent a small body of his cavalry to inform the chief that the Spanish leader was near, and soon presented himself before the proud Mobilian. He was found seated upon two cushions, on a large and elegant matting, and on a natural eminence 'which commanded a delightful prospect.'

General Woodward disputes some of these locations of Indian

12

towns with the following excerpt from his letter.

> It was in Talladega that the Tallassees lived; and it must have been at that point where the invitation from Tuscaloosa was received by DeSoto. I have remarked somewhere long before this that the Tuckabatchy town, on Tallapoosa, was settled at least two centuries before the Tallasees settled the town that they left in 1836.

Returning to the Portuguese narrative:

> His address of welcome was very short. De Soto's reply was conciliatory. A large pack horse was selected of sufficient strength to carry the huge frame of Tuskaloosa, and side by side, the Spanish leader and the Indian ruler, journeyed toward Maubila.

> They crossed the Alabama, marched over what is now the county of Wilcox, passed October 17, through populous towns well stored with corn, beans, pumpkins, and other provisions, which may have been the eastern part of the present county of Clarke.

> De Soto was suspicious in regard to the intentions of Tuskaloosa so before daylight on the morning of October 18, 1540, at the head of one hundred horsemen and one hundred footmen, he took the haughty Chief with him and marched rapidly southward. This proved to be for the Maubilians and Spaniards alike, an eventful day.

> The trail was lined with towns, villages, and hamlets. At eight in the morning they reached the town, the capital of Tuskaloosa's dominion. It is described as situated on a beautiful plain, beside a river, a river large in the eyes of Spaniards, containing eighty handsome houses, each capable of holding a thousand men. They were built doubtless of wood, but few of the Spaniards had an opportunity to examine them minutely, and no special description seems to have been given, except that these houses all fronted on a

13

large public square.

The town was surrounded by a high wall made of the trunks of trees, set firmly in the ground, side by side, additional strength being given by cross timbers, and by large vines interlacing the upright trunks. The whole wood work is said to have been covered with a mud plaster, which resembled handsome masonry.

Port holes were arranged in this wall, and towers, sufficiently large to hold eight men, were constructed, one hundred and fifty feet apart. There were only two gates, the one opened toward the east and the other toward the west.

Into the great public square of this walled town, on the morning already named. Tuskaloosa and De Soto entered, about two hours after sunrise, 'amid songs and music from Indian flutes, while beautiful brown girls danced gracefully before them.'

Dismounting from their horses, the two leaders were seated together for a short time under a canopy, when Tuskaloosa, not receiving a satisfactory reply to a request which he had made, left De Soto and went into one of the large houses.

It seems that De Soto, although an invited visitor at this town, had treated the Indian Chief as a hostage, and restrained his personal freedom. This had incensed the Chief and from the house in his own capital, where he had sought relief from the presence of De Soto, he refused to return to take breakfast with the Spaniards. He suggested to the Spanish interpreter, that it would be well for his Chief to remove his forces from that territory.

De Soto perceived that danger was near, and instructed his men to be ready for conflict A disturbance soon began. A Spaniard discovered that more than ten thousand warriors were in the houses, abundantly supplied with clubs and stones, with bows and arrows; that the old women and

14

children had been sent away; and that the Indians were designing to capture the two hundred Spaniards and De Soto.

Little time was given for that morning's meal. An Indian drew a bow upon a group of Spaniards, then a Spanish soldier struck him down with his sword,. The red streams of blood began to flow. De Soto had the first bloody encounter, but it was brief. From among more than ten thousand enraged warriors, De Soto at the head of his men, fighting hand to hand, led his little band outside the gate into the adjoining plain.

His cavalry rushed for their horses, tied outside the walls which the Indians had already begun to kill. Retreating from the Indians, the Spanish leader halted some distance out upon the plain.

By this time the Indian burden bearers of the expedition had arrived with nearly all the baggage and hurried inside the town. Having thus captured and disposed of the baggage and camp equipment, the excited warriors crowded without the gate tilled the air with their exulting shouts.

This seems to have aroused the martial fury of the Spaniards. De Soto at the head of his hundred horsemen, followed by the footmen, charged furiously upon the Indians, and drove them again within the gate. But from the port holes and towers the missiles of the Indians drove the Spaniards back from the walls again into the plain.

Again, the Maubilians rushed outside the gate, or dropped from the walls, and fought fiercely, but vainly with Spanish swords and lances they were killed. Now and then small parties of fresh horsemen arrived and plunged at once into the thick of the fight. Three hours thus passed with terrible slaughter, one side receding and again advancing, clubs and arrows and bare flesh, forming but a poor defense against burnished steel, Spanish lances, and charging war-horses,

15

when at length the Maubilians re-entered their walled town and closed behind them the heavy gates.

Mid-day passed, and the sun of that day seemed to be nearing the lofty tree tops when the last of De Soto's forces under Moscoso, his camp-master, arrived. De Soto should have retired and left these natives of the soil in possession of their strong walled town, but such was not the custom of Spanish adventurers in American wilds, and his baggage and camp equipment were within, so more blood flowed and more carnage followed.

Uniting all his force, forming his best armed footmen into four divisions for storming the walls, and armed with bucklers for defense and battle-axes for assault, a charge was made. The gates were at length forced open and the mortar broken from the walls.

Those ponderous battle-axes had before this day made impressions upon well defended European castles, and it could not be expected that Indian woodwork or masonry would withstand the assault of desperate and infuriated trained knights and warriors.

De Soto's soldiers rushed into the enclosed square and horrible destruction was again resumed. The horsemen remained without to cut off all retreat, and the merciless Spaniards commenced the work of extermination. Often, it is said, the brave Maubilians drove the Spaniards outside the walls, but as often they returned with renewed impetuosity.

The young Maubilian girls who danced so gracefully in the morning, fought and fell beside the bravest Indian warriors. At length De Soto, wounded and infuriated, passed out of the gate once more, mounted his war-horse, returned, and charged through the Indian ranks. Others followed his example. The fearful work of death went on. Coats of mail and bucklers protected the Spaniards from many fatal wounds, while their sharp swords and well tempered lances made terrible havoc upon muscle unprotected by shield or breast-plate or heavy clothing.

The day drew to a close. The conflict had been fought for over nine hours. Then the houses were set on fire. Amid flame and smoke, the fearful carnage was near its end. "The sun went down, far to the westward, beyond other and greater rivers which Spaniards had not yet seen.

Maubilia was in ruins, and her inhabitants destroyed. The number slain was estimated by one chronicler at eleven thousand. Historian Albert Picket suggests six thousand as the lowest estimate.

This disastrous day decided not alone the fate of a mighty Indian tribe. It decided also De Soto's destiny. He lost eighty-two soldiers and forty-five horses, his valuable equipment and baggage, including camp furniture, instruments, clothes, books, medicines, the gathered pearls, the holy relics and the priestly robes, the flour, the wine, and nearly everything of value brought from the ships. One surgeon alone survived, and there were seventeen hundred wounds to dress.

Although he learned that his vessels were awaiting him in Pensacola Bay, "so thoroughly had many of the cavaliers become disheartened that they had determined to desert him and his cause when they reached the coast; and thus De Soto was obliged to change his plans."

After a month's delay while wounds were healing and provisions collected including "a number of Maubilian women of incomparable beauty" were brought into the camp. DeSoto, "in desperate sullenness," led his disheartened troops into the northern and western wilderness instead of planting a colony "in that beautiful region in the heart of Spanish Florida" which is now Alabama.

The troops had expected to march southward toward the coast, and it was questionable whether they would, but De Soto threatened to put to death the first man who should show that he wished to go toward the ships, and although the order to march northward took the cavaliers by surprise, none refused obedience, and on-ward to a dark destiny the ill-fated expedition began again its course.

Passing northward through a fertile region now known as the counties of Clarke, and Marengo, and Greene, "like a thunder-cloud which has brought destruction to fields and forest, the sullen Spaniards crossed the Black Warrior and entered what is now the state of Mississippi." They spent the winter among the Chickasaws.

In April, 1541, they resumed their march toward the northwest, now numbering less than seven hundred men, and about one hundred horses. In May of that year they reached the "Father of Waters," the Mississippi, and crossed that mighty current, wandered over trackless wilds, then returned to the Mississippi in May of 1542.

De Soto's work as a warrior, an explorer and leader was over. He found no gold region, conquered no mighty empire, and was not to outrank Cortez and Pizarro in giving provinces to Spain. He was "no more to mount the war-horse, his right arm would wield the sword and hurl the lance no longer, he had fought his last battle, and a slow, malignant fever soon terminated his stormy career.

De Soto closed his eyes in death when he had no superior in command upon the whole broad continent, and his body sunk to its last resting-place in the channel of that "majestic river the discovery of which is inseparably connected with his name."

The remnant of De Soto's army, numbered three hundred and fifty was under the command of Moscoso. In July of 1543, having with great effort constructed seven brigantines, "embarked upon that broad and rapid river, and kept with them "the beautiful women of Maubilia." In September they reached Spanish settlements in Mexico, and sent to Cuba the tidings of De Soto's fate.

Again, General Thomas Simpson Woodward sheds some doubt on the accuracy of the Portuguese narrative as to the location of this famous battle. He states in his letter August 12, 1858 letter:

18

The Creek Indians say they once had a giant chief called Tustanugga Lusta or Black Warrior. But Tuscaloosa is a mixed word of Creek and Choctaw. Tusca is Creek, and signifies a warrior — Loosa is Choctaw, and-signifies black. But whether it was this man that fought DeSoto, I never heard; but have always understood that at Thlea Walla (now in Blount County, Georgia) was the place they fought.....And why I am better satisfied that the Maubila fight took its origin from the Thlea Walla fight, is that there were but few remains of Indian settlements on the Alabama river below the mouth of Cahawba, and they were very small.

Archaeologists have looked for Mabila for many years without much luck. The specific location of the Battle of Maubilla has never been found. "A conference bringing a variety of scholars together was held in 2006 and published as The Search For Mabila in 2009 (Knight 2009). A consensus from that conference found that Mabila is likely to be somewhere in southern Alabama, on the Alabama river or its tributaries within a few miles of Selma."

The location of Maubilla along with other questions concerning De Soto's route through the southeastern United States remains a mystery.

French Explorers

First Mardi Gras In America

New Orleans, Louisiana has long been held the Mardi Gras city in America, but Mardi Gras was not celebrated openly in New Orleans until the 1730s. The first Mardi Gras celebration in America actually had its beginning in Mobile, Alabama.

The first white settlement in Alabama occurred in 1702 at Fort Louis De La Mobile, near the present city of Mobile. Though De Soto traveled through Alabama earlier, no permanent white settlement had ever been established by him. France wanted to gain a foothold in the new World and in 1699 Pierre LeMoyne Sieur D'iberville began to explore Mobile Bay.

They landed on an island, now the Gulf Coast of Alabama, where they were sickened by the appalling discovery of a mountain of bones of Indians, men and women—many with their heads cut off. They named the island Isle Du Massacre or Massacre Island because of this macabre scene and wondered what matter of inhabitants existed on such a place.

Actually, the mountain of bones was just a burial mound that had broken open during a hurricane, but it horrified the crew so much that they set sail up the Mobile River and entered the Mississippi/Alabama/Louisiana Delta Gulf Coast Region.

D'Iberville declared his camp 'Pointe du Mardi Gras.' He eventually settled near Twenty-Seven Mile Bluff where Fort Louis De La Mobile was built. The colony was part of Louisiana at the time and consisted of only thirty families.

A catholic church was built in 1704, the first in Alabama, and the same year the first white child, Claude Jousette, was born in Mobile.

Also in the same year, Fort Louis De La Mobile was formally made the capital of the French province of Louisiana. Masque De La Mobile (Mardi Gras) was celebrated at Fort Louis De La Mobile until

1709. Mardi Gras began as a holiday for French colonists to remember their homeland roots.

D'Iberville died of yellow fever while in Cuba in 1706 and his younger brother Bienville Lemoyne became governor of the area. In 1797, the name Massacre Island was changed to the more respectable name of Dauphin in honor of the heir to the French throne. At this time the little island was the capital of the whole Louisiana Territory which made up about two-thirds of the United States. Today this island is the beautiful resort town of Dauphin Island.

A granite cross erected by the Colonial Dames of Alabama near Dauphin Street bears the inscription: "To Jean Baptiste La money, Sieur de Bienville. Native of Montreal, Canada. Naval Office of France, Governor of Louisiana and founder of its first capital, Mobile, 1711

However, the men of the settlement still faced a big problem. There was a shortage of women. France came up with a solution and the

24

famous 'cassette girls' immigrated to Alabama to become wives of the colonists.

Cassette girls

They were named cassette girls because the French government gave each volunteer some clothing and a small trunk called a 'cassette' to take with them to America. On arrival they soon found mates among the male colonists.

In about 1713, Fort Dauphin was moved to a location in Mobile due to flooding and Bienville Lemoyne proclaimed a Societé de Saint Louise Holiday in Mobile which was the beginning of what one day would be the world famous and popular Mardi Gras.

The French explored inland as far as Madison County, Alabama by 1715 because a French map shows a French fort on the Tennessee River close to where Muscle Shoals is today.

Antoine De La Mothe, Sieur De Cadillac arrived aboard a French frigate in Mobile Bay on May 17, 1713 and became Governor of the Louisiana Province. He had previously settled Fort Ponchartrain du

Detroit, the beginning of Detroit, Michigan in 1701. The Cadillac automobile is named after him.

Alabama Belonged To France
For Sixty-five Years

For sixty-five years the French held the territory which now includes Alabama. The population of their colony in 1712 was about four hundred. In 1713 officers of Crozat, a rich Paris merchant, received from the French king a charter of this colony from the French king and took possession of the territory.

He established trading and military posts at the head of the Alabama, near the union of the Coosa and Tallapoosa; "at the mouth of the Cahawba; at Jones' Bluff on the Tombeckbee; at the site of St. Stephens; at Nashville, on the Cumberland; and at the Muscle Shoals on the Tennessee then called the Cherokee."

The Alabama waters began to be navigated by Frenchmen, and into the ancient forests French soldiers and traders and adventurers penetrated. The Native Americans between the rivers saw the white men come and go, and probably remembered the accounts their grandfathers had given concerning white and bearded strangers when De Soto had visited long ago. From that time onward they had abundant cause to remember the white man.

Noted Historian Alexander Beaufort Meek, who came with his family on a 46 day journey to Tuscaloosa, Alabama in 1819, stated: "The French traders and missionaries were ever bold, adventurous and enterprising, and it is not extravagant to say that every inch of our territory was trod by their feet, if not watered by their blood before 1763."

Near the center of the state, in current day Elmore County, Alabama, a fort was built and given the name of Ft. Toulouse in 1714. Fort St. Stephens was probably established about the same time in present day Washington County and Fort Tombeckbee, (Tombigbee) two hundred and fifty miles above Mobile, was established in 1736.

British traders from the Carolinas arrived in Alabama before 1714 and penetrated these same wilds. They traded with many of the Indian tribes and carried on a lucrative traffic. However, French and British interests in Alabama as elsewhere in the world, came into conflict.

"The few French inhabitants along the Bay, on the banks of Mobile river, and at old St. Stephens, were too far removed from the English colonies of the coast to enter actively into these conflicts. They loved ease and pleasure; they found a delightful climate and wild game in abundance. "

The French formed alliances with and sometimes married the Native American maidens and engaged in trade with the Native Americans. Eventually they opened plantations and cultivated rice, tobacco, and indigo. Their plantations extended up the Tensaw and Mobile rivers and included many of the islands in these rivers. The first island below the union of the Tombigbee and Alabama contained the plantation of the Chevalier de Lucre.

The first Christian marriages were solemnized in 1704, when the twenty-three girls (the Cassette Girls) sent to Mobile from France found husbands in a few days. At the same time four priests and four Sisters of Charity came to the new territory. The Roman Catholic religion was established, and priests and friars were soon sent among the neighboring tribes.

Failing to make money by traffic and discouraged by the hostility of the Indians especially of the Chickasaws, Crozat surrendered his charter in 1717. The French population around this time was about eight hundred. The French made settlements in what is now Mississippi, at Natchez and upon the Yazoo river and founded New Orleans in 1718. The name Mississippi soon become well known in France between 1716 and 1720. It is often mentioned with the expression, 'Mississippi Bubble.'

The Mississippi Bubble Burst

John Law, a native of Edinburgh, was a celebrated financier, who had established a bank in France in 1716 by authority of King, Louis XV. It was made up of twelve hundred shares, each share being three thousand livres. A French livre was equal to eighteen and a half cents at the time. One share was equal to $555. This bank became the office for all public receipts.

In 1718 the Western or India Company, an association chartered the year before to manage the territory of Louisiana, was annexed to this bank. The Company had a capital of one hundred thousand livres. That same year, the bank was declared to be a royal bank, and the shares soon "rose to twenty times their original value." Many people were suddenly rich, "on paper," from the French king and in Paris as well as all over France, expensive living and wild speculation followed. This time of wild speculation did not last and as with all bubbles, it burst two years later.

The bank shares sunk in value "as rapidly as they had risen, occasioning great and widespread financial distress and bankruptcy." Multitudes were financially ruined, and distress was felt all over France.

During these few years of supposed wealth and prosperity, great activity was manifested in "promoting emigration to the Louisiana territory." Many slaves were brought from the coast of Africa and placed upon the French plantations.

In 1720, two hundred and sixty colonists came for the grant of St. Catherine near Natchez, two hundred and forty for the grant of Lonore, and in 1721 three hundred came for the grant of Madame Chaumont at Pascagoula, two hundred German emigrants for the grant of Law on the Arkansas, and in June 1722, two hundred and fifty more Germans came. The last vessel brought news of the failure of that great royal bank.

John Law Camp 1720 Biloxi, Mississippi

When the Western Company was operating, wealth was supposed to be growing in their hands, and more than seven thousand colonists settled in various parts of the territory of Louisiana. However when the Mississippi Bubble burst, this area was so neglected that settlers lacked the essential necessities to simply survive.

The seat of government for the colony was removed from Mobile to New Orleans in 1723 when the population in New Orleans reached two hundred. The families first lived in a hundred huts and cabins. The French province was divided into nine civil and military districts. These districts were:

- Alabama
- Mobile
- Biloxi
- New Orleans
- Natchez
- Yazoo
- Illinois
- Wabash
- Arkansas
- Natchitoches

Around this time, the French took Pensacola from the Spaniards.

Faced with failure in 1732, the Western Company surrendered their charter to their king. At the time, the population was around five thousand whites and two thousand slaves.

Bienville, again Governor under the king, made an expedition against the Chickasaws in 1736, passing up the Tombigbee with boats of various kinds, and with "French, Indian, and colored troops, in all fifteen hundred men." They had munitions of war with them. Faced with hostile Indians and many other difficulties, his venture was unsuccessful so he returned to Mobile a disappointed man. The French crossed and recrossed the Alabama and Tombigbee rivers, but seemed to have made no additional settlements.

In 1733, some French traders and English traders from the Georgia colony, penetrated the wilds among the Indian tribes of the Southeast, furnished them with European articles, learned the trails and river fords and formed alliances with Indian princesses and beautiful daughters of powerful chiefs.

They gave rise to a class of border men, or *country men*, Native Americans with the blood of whites flowing through their veins, who became, "men of renown," noted warriors in battle, wealthy traders, shrewd diplomatists, strong friends and dangerous enemies.

In 1752, the Marquis de Vaudreuil, formerly governor of Canada, went up the Tombigbee again with a fleet of boats of French troops and Choctaw warriors The Choctaws were against the Chickasaws. He was also unsuccessful in settling in the Indian territory and returned to Mobile leaving the Indians in the center of the future State of Alabama still unconquered.

In 1754, the bloody French and Indian war began in America and was declared in Europe between Great Britain and France.

The Seven-Years War, commenced in 1756 and ended in 1763. It resulted in the exile of seven thousand peaceful Acadian French peasants of Nova Scotia. Some of those exiled Acadians settled in West Florida.

Revolutionary War

Alabama's First Indian Agents

James Seagrove, born in Ireland, was the first Indian Agent among the Creeks. He served until the appointment of the commissioners in 1796.

David Brodie Mitchell was born near Nuthill Perthshire. Scotland on October 22, 1766 and died at Milledgeville, Georgia, April 22, 1837. He was a state senator from Baldwin County and governor of Georgia, 1809-13. He served as Indian agent for two years, but was removed on account of irregularities in office.

After the report of the commissioners in 1796, Colonel Benjamin Hawkins, a member of President George Washington's staff, was appointed Agent of Indian Affairs.

Colonel Benjamin Hawkins

Colonel Benjamin Hawkins was born in Warren County, North Carolina August 15, 1754 and died June 6, 1816. He was a delegate in the Continental Congress, and a senator from North Carolina. He served until 1816 when he died at the Agency, in Crawford County, Georgia. Philemon Hawkins, a son of Colonel Benjamin Hawkins, and Sub-Agent to the Creeks is shown in the Official Register of 1816 as Acting Agent. He was stationed at Fort Hawkins on Okmulgee River opposite the city of Macon.

The next Indian Agent was John Crowell. He was born in Halifax County, North Carolina in 1785.

Tomb of Col. John Crowell 1935 in Russell County, Alabama

He served as territorial delegate from the Alabama Territory, and

36

was the first congressman from the state of Alabama. He was appointed by James Monroe as Creek Indian Agent in 1821.

He removed the agency from the Flint River site, Georgia, to Fort Mitchell, in Russell County, Alabama, and served until the removal of the Indians to the west in 1838. He died at his home at Fort Mitchell, June 25, 1846.

General T. S. Woodward said of John Crowell: "He sleeps upon Fort Mitchell hill, where rests a crowd that no man need be ashamed to be picked up with. in a coming day."

The administration of Crowell was wrought with numerous contentions. During its early years, controversies arose between Governor Troup of Georgia, the U. S. Government, the Lower Creeks, and Colonel Crowell, the Agent, caused by certain treaties and land sessions which were made contrary to the wishes of the majority of the Nation.

Later a controversy between South Carolina Conference of the Methodist Church, the Baptist Missionaries, and the Agent arose, and it became necessary for the Secretary of War to order an investigation. The difficulties were settled amicably.

Royalists Settle In Alabama

Before the 1760's the eastern bank of the Mississippi River was inhabited mostly by Native Americans. Starting in 1768, British West Florida began issuing land grants to settlers and speculators.

Once English control was extended over the area of Alabama, the Natchez region and the western part of the present state of Mississippi attracted many settlers. They came from the Atlantic colonies in considerable numbers.

The Mississippi river and its eastern tributaries seemed to be at first the most attractive for settlement. From the Atlantic colonies, first from Roanoke in North Carolina, as early as 1764, then from South Carolina, Georgia, Virginia, and New Jersey, large numbers came, either in boats down the tributary rivers, or cutting a pathway through the wilderness. They made settlements extending some twenty miles east of the river. Some early groups included:

- A small German settlement was upon the Pascagoola, a river in the southeastern part of Mississippi.

- In 1767 a colony of French Protestants, in number two hundred and nine, made a settlement upon the Escambia river north of Pensacola. They received a large grant of land from King George III and were sent across the ocean at royal expense. They built white cottages among the live oak groves, and erected a church building with one simple village spire. This colony was not long afterward desolated by the yellow fever, "the scourge of the tropics."

- Scottish Highlanders came from North Carolina and settled thirty miles east of Natchez. In 1770, and again in 1778, many immigrants came by the way of the Ohio river from New Jersey, and Virginia, and Delaware. Immigrants also began to come from Great Britain and the British West Indies.

39

- The outbreak of the American Revolution brought many Tories and Loyalists to the area. Most of them were trying to escape the war and settled on the fertile soils of Natchez.

By 1775, there was approximately 2500 people along the eastern banks between Walnut Hills (present day Vicksburg) and Manchac on the Iberville River..

"It does not appear that in these years many additions were made to the settlers on the Mobile and Tensaw rivers. The plantations opened there must, however, have been productive, and business enterprise was evidently not stagnant, for in 1772 the exports from Mobile and Pensacola were, according to Pickett "indigo, raw-hides, corn, fine cattle, tallow, rice, pitch, bear's oil, tobacco, tar, squared timber, indigo seed, myrtle wax, cedar-posts and planks, salted wild beef, pecan nuts, cypress and pine-boards, plank of various woods, shingles, dried salt-fish, scantling, sassafras, canes, staves and heading hoops, oranges and peltry."

The cultivation of cotton had also started, and some small machines were invented for separating the lint from the seed. "The French planters had some machines by which, it is said by Captain Barnard Roman, in his *Florida* "seventy pounds of clear cotton can be made every day." Whitney's Cotton Gin was not invented until 1792.

Pensacola, the capital of the province, contained in 1771 about one hundred and eighty houses built of wood. It was the seat of government and the first place of traffic for the coming settlers. The French houses of the wealthy in Mobile were of brick.

In 1775, the Thirteen United Colonies had a population of about three million people that extended from New Hampshire to Georgia, and were "entering upon that great conflict with the Mother Country, the American Revolution."

West Florida did not enter this conflict. Therefore it was a secure retreat for the Royalists of the Carolinas and Georgia, who held themselves still loyal to the king of Great Britain. The banks of that river, then called Tombeckbee, (Tombigbee) became attractive to this large class of adventurers and refugees.

"In the year 1777 an English botanist, William Bartram, visited the settled parts of West Florida. He found on the Tensaw river many well-cultivated plantations on which settlers were living. His route both going and coming seems to have been on the east side of the Alabama. From him, therefore, nothing is learned concerning settlers on the west side."

William Bartram

"Near the northern boundary of the province and still beside the river, Bartram's party met with some Georgians, a man and his wife, some young children, one young woman and three young men, packing their goods on a dozen horses-who were on their way to settle upon the Alabama river, a few miles above its union with the Tombeckbee."

According to Historian Albert Pickett, these "are believed to have been among the first Anglo-Americans who settled in the present Baldwin county. That some such settler had already reached the Tombeckbee (Tombigbee) is quite certain, so that we may safely place the commencement of what became permanent American settlement as early as the year 1777."

James Willing And His Band Left A Trail Of Devastation Seldom Equaled

By the time of the American Revolution white men loyal to the Crown lived in two small settlements of the British Province of West Florida. The settlements were on the Gulf Coast and Natchez, Mississippi. Being situated so far south, they would have felt little of the struggle for Independence if not for a daring raid of a man named James Willing and his band of Americans who traveled down the Mississippi River in 1778.

Spain had possessed the port of New Orleans since 1763, and the Fort was fortified as far north as St. Louis. Spain was willing to embarrass the British so they offered assistance to the Americans through their port of New Orleans via the work of Oliver Pollock, an American merchant who resided in New Orleans.

Oliver Pollock, a merchant and a financier of the American Revolutionary War, met with Spanish governors of Louisiana Luis de Unzaga and Bernalde de Galvez and acted as an agent for the Continental Army and Governor Patrick Henry of Virginia.

In 1776 an American Revolutionary soldier, Captain George Gibson, came down the Mississippi River with eighteen men from Fort Pitt. Governor Luis De Unzaga provided the Americans with ten thousand pounds of gunpowder. Gibson voluntarily surrendered to a temporary arrest to avoid alerting the British of the transaction while his Chief Assistant William Linn returned upstream with the powder.

Meanwhile, Oliver Pollock continued to urge his friends to support an American expedition down the Mississippi River like the one launched against the Canadians in 1775-1776. He finally convinced his friend, James Willing, who had been residing in Natchez since 1772, to return to Pennsylvania and encourage Congress to send troops down the Mississippi River.

Congress had been debating the idea to send fifteen hundred men under the command of Colonel George Morgan to seize the Mississippi settlements from England, but they rejected the plan.

James Willing, Robert Morris of Pennsylvania and Oliver Pollock finally persuaded the secret committee of the War Board to a more scaled down version of the original plan.

Soon afterward, a strange group led by James Willing raided the Natchez district. Although, he was evidently only authorized to bring back five boat loads of supplies, he was unofficially allowed to plunder Tory property along the way, and dispose of it in New Orleans.

January 11, 1778, Captain Willing along with twenty-nine men, left Fort Pitt in the U.S.S. Rattletrap. He recruited additional men along the way and in early February, when he stopped at the mouth of the Arkansas, he had one hundred men.

An advance party, led by Lieutenant Thomas McIntire, surprised and captured four British Indian agents who were being entertained at the home of John Watkins, a Walnut Hills planter. The group proceeded downstream to seize the persons and property of Anthony Hutchins and William McIntosh. Captain Willing considered them both leading Tories in the community of Natchez.

"Frightened by the unexpected appearance of an armed force in their territory, the inhabitants of Natchez authorized four prominent planters to arrange favorable terms of capitulation with Willing in order to avert further disaster. On February 21, the American captain accepted their offer not to take up arms against the United States or to assist any of its enemies in exchange for his promise to protect their property as long as they remained neutral in the war. During his brief stay in Natchez, Willing persuaded a number of the settlers who were sympathetic to the American cause to join his force."

Around the same time of the Natchez invasion, an advance group under McIntire's command was on its way down the Mississippi with Anthony Hutchins and most of his slaves in custody. They were concealed by a dense early morning fog and managed to surprise and capture the *Rebecca*, an English vessel, anchored to the river bank at Manchac. They then sent out small detachments of men to search the countryside for slaves and property of known Tories. McIntire awaited the appearance of Willing from Natchez and Oliver Pollock's nephew, Thomas Pollock, from New Orleans.

Further to the North, Willing's larger force plundered the property of Tories in the Baton Rouge area. A few settlers had some advanced warning of Willing's approach and managed to escape into Spanish territory, but most of the inhabitants were taken by surprise.

Before he left, Willing and his 'Troop of Rascals,' as one disgruntled settler described them, left a trail of devastation seldom equaled in the annals of western history. As another inhabitant expressed it, in somewhat of an exaggerated fashion, there was "nothing to be seen but destruction and desolation."

William Dunbar, perhaps the most prominent planter in the vicinity, was particularly vivid in his description of the havoc wrought by Willing's men. "All was fish that came into their nett," he wrote. They spared nothing. They seized "all my waring apparel, bed and table linen," Dunbar recalled "not a shirt was left in the house— blankets, pieces of cloth, sugar, silver ware."

Miraculously, no one was killed, although there were a few narrow escapes. One British Indian agent was "obliged to fly in his night shirt to the Spanish Fort at Manchac". He was barely ahead of his determined pursuers. Rumor had it that the Americans planned to slice Henry Alexander "into a hundred pieces and to flay Alexander Ross alive when they captured him."

Fortunately, both men remained a step in front of Willing's band. Although Dunbar and the other victims refused to admit it at the time, Willing was not completely indiscriminate in his choice of victims to plunder. Those known to be sympathetic to the American cause were spared the same fate met by those who were outspoken

British partisans.

While Willing was busy plundering the property of British settlers around Baton Rouge, Oliver Pollock was preparing Governor Galvez for his expected arrival in New Orleans.

Galvez declared Willing's men refugees, granted them asylum in Louisiana and permitted them to purchase supplies in New Orleans, including weapons. He also, extended to Willing the use of several public buildings as barracks for his troops. Finally, and most important of all, he allowed Willing to dispose of the booty at public auction. "These sales eventually netted the Americans more than $62,000."

The American Revolution Was Fought In Alabama

When the American Revolution comes to mind, most people think of the Eastern seaboard, but the war raged from Georgia north to Maine. It may be surprising to know that a Revolutionary War battle took place in the heart of what is now downtown Mobile, Alabama.

"The Battle of Fort Charlotte was fought from March 10-13, 1780 for control of a sixty year old fort on the waterfront of the former French city. It was one of two significant Alabama battles of the Revolution and opened the door for the British defeat on the Gulf Coast. Remembered today as the Battle of Fort Charlotte, the engagement was an important part of General Bernado de Galvez' Gulf Coast campaign.

Jean-Baptiste Le Moyne de Bienville

Mobile was originally founded, by Jean-Baptiste Le Moyne de Bienville, in 1702 as Fort Louis de la Mobile at 27 Mile Bluff up river. After the Mobile River flooded and damaged the fort, Mobile was relocated in 1711 to the current site. A temporary wooden stockade fort was constructed named Fort Louis after the old fort up river. In 1723, construction of a new brick fort with a stone foundation began. It was later renamed as Fort Condé in honor of King Louis XIV's brother.

By the Treaty of Paris, February 10, 1763, when West Florida became a British possession, Major Robert Farmer was placed in command of the Mobile district. By 1763, when the British took over after the French and Indian War, the fort was in ruins. It was renamed Fort Charlotte, in compliment to the young queen of England.

Little interest was shown in Fort Charlotte for many years, owing perhaps to the bad health of the place. In March, 1771, the fort underwent many repairs. However, in June of that year Haldimand removed twelve 12-pounders from Fort Charlotte to Pensacola, replacing them with small pieces.

While it was repaired at that time, by the time hostilities with Spain neared in 1779, it was again in disrepair. The garrison's regulars were primarily from the 60th regiment, and were augmented by Loyalists from Maryland and Pennsylvania, as well as local volunteers, in total about three hundred men.

When Spain entered the American Revolutionary War in 1779 Bernado de Galvez, the governor of Spanish Louisiana, began offensive operations. In September 1779 he gained complete control over the lower Mississippi River by capturing Fort Bute and then shortly thereafter obtaining the surrender of the remaining forces following the Battle of Baton Rouge. Following these successes, he began planning operations against Mobile and Pensacola, the remaining British presence in the province of West Florida.

In 1780, Galvez, made an attack upon Mobile. Galvez had assembled a mixed force of Spanish regulars and militia in New Orleans. While he had requested additional troops from Havana in 1779, his requests were rejected.

Before departing New Orleans, he dispatched one of his lieutenants to Havana to make one last request and on January 11, 1780, a fleet of twelve ships carrying seven hundred and fifty-four men set sail, They reached the mouth of the Mississippi on January 18 and they were joined on January 20 by the American ship, *West Florida*, under the command of Captain Pickles and with a crew of fifty-eight. On February 6, a hurricane scattered the fleet. In spite of this, all ships arrived outside Mobile Bay by February 9.

The fleet encountered significant problems getting into the bay. Several ships ran aground on sand bars and at least one, the *Volante*, was wrecked as a result. Galvez salvaged guns from the wreck and set them up on Mobile Point to guard the bay entrance.

On February 20, reinforcements arrived from Havana bringing the force to about twelve hundred men. By February 25, the Spanish had landed their army on the shores of the Dog River, about 10 miles from Fort Charlotte. They were informed by a deserter that the fort was garrisoned by three hundred men.

News of Galvez success reached Mobile, where Elias Durnford, commander of Fort Charlotte, had been directing improvements to the fort's defenses with a garrison of only two hundred and seventy-nine soldiers, the minister, commissary, surgeon's mate, and about fifty-two black servants. Galvez sent a letter to Elias Durnford on March 1, offering to accept his surrender which Durnford politely rejected. Galvez began setting up gun batteries around Fort Charlotte.

Durnford wrote to General John Campbell at Pensacola for reinforcements. On March 5 and 6, most of the Pensacola garrison left on a march toward Mobile, but because of delays crossing rivers, they could not arrive in time to assist the besieged fort.

In anticipation of the battle, Durnford torched the city of Mobile to prevent its houses and shops from being used as cover by the attacking army. It was a wasted gesture that caused enormous suffering for the inhabitants of the city. While the Spanish engaged in siege operations to move their guns nearer the fort, Galvez and

Durnford exchanged a courteous written dialogue. Galvez politely criticized Durnford for burning houses in order to deny the cover they provided to the Spaniards.

Durnford responded by pointing out that the other side of the fort (away from most of the town) offered a better vantage point for attack. All the while, the Spanish continued to dig trenches and bombard the fort. On March 13, the walls of Fort Charlotte were breached, and Durnford surrendered his garrison the next day.

Galvez did not immediately move against Pensacola after his victory at Fort Charlotte, although he wanted to take advantage of the British disorganization caused by the attempt to support Mobile. However, since he knew that Pensacola was strongly defended, and armed with powerful cannons, he again requested large-scale naval support from Havana. He learned in April that additional reinforcements, including British Navy vessels, arrived at Pensacola. Without reinforcements, he left a garrison in Mobile for Havana to raise the troops and equipment needed for an attack on Pensacola.

Galvez did not actually launch his successful attack on Pensacola until 1781, and then only after the garrison at Mobile fended of a counterattack by the British in January 1781.

From 1780 to 1813, Spain ruled the region, and the fort was renamed Fort Carlota. In 1813, Mobile was occupied by United States troops, and the fort was renamed again as Fort Charlotte

During French, British and Spanish rule, Fort Charlotte had been the important center of Mobile life, but when Florida became a part of the United States, and Mobile was growing up around the Fort, there was a feeling that it should be torn down and the ground be converted into city lots.

Although Major-General Bernard on December 23, 1817, made report to the U. S. chief engineer that of all the forts in Louisiana, Fort Charlotte was the only one well built, and recommended it be retained, the sale of the old Fort was authorized by act of Congress, April 20, 1818. This act was not carried into effect, however, and it remained garrisoned until 1820. The sale actually took place in October, 1820, much of the property going to a syndicate, calling itself the Mobile Lot Company.

In 1820, the U.S. Congress authorized sale and removal of the fort because it was no longer needed for defense. Later, city funds paid for the demolition to allow new streets built eastward towards the river and southward. By late 1823, most of the above-ground traces of Mobile's fort were gone, leaving only underground structures.

Fort Condé and its surrounding buildings covered about 11 acres. It was constructed of local brick and stone, with earthen dirt walls, plus cedar wood. A crew of twenty black slaves and five white workmen performed original work on the fort.

Map of Mobile 1725 showing Fort Fort Condé

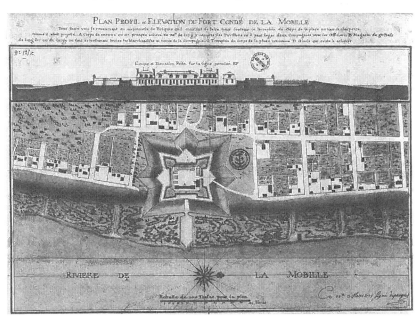

Fort Condé guarded Mobile and its citizens for almost one hundred years, from 1723-1820. The fort had been built by the French to defend against British or Spanish attack on the location of Mobile and its bay as a port to the Gulf of Mexico, on the eastern most part of the French Louisiana colony. The importance of Mobile and Fort Condé was significant. The fort protected access into the strategic region between the Mississippi River and the Atlantic colonies along the Alabama River and Tombigbee River.

Fort Condé, located in Mobile, Alabama, at 150 South Royal Street, is a reconstruction, at 4/5 scale, as a third of the original 1720s French Fort Condé/Fort Charlotte/Fort Carlota site. If the fort had been reconstructed full-size, today it would cover large sections of Royal Street, Government Boulevard, Church, St. Emanuel, and Theatre Streets in downtown Mobile.

Early Immigrants
To Alabama

The Wife Of President Andrew Jackson, Was A Pioneer Of Madison County, Alabama

As early as 1777, some expeditionary trips by hopeful settlers were made through what is now Madison County in north Alabama. Thomas Hutchins led a group into what was then the "Indian Territory" through Madison County towards Muscle Shoals. However, the Native Americans attacked and drove them from the area.

Revolutionary War Soldier, General James Robertson with eight others had settled at Nashville, Tennessee and in the fall they returned to east Tennessee for their families. Colonel John Donelson led a band of some one hundred and sixty persons along the Tennessee River to settle where Nashville, Tennessee stands today. Some of the men in the party were James Cain, Isaac Neely, Benjamin Porter, John White and John Cotton.

General Robertson proceeded first, with a number of young men to raise the necessary buildings. Colonel John Donelson followed with another party of emigrants, including the women and children.

Colonel John Donelson conceived the idea of reaching the new settlement by water to avoid the toil and peril of the route through the wilderness. They traveled down the Tennessee and up the Cumberland rivers.

"No man, white or red, had ever attempted the voyage, which was really more dangerous than the overland route, while there were equally as many Indians to be encountered. At the suck, one of the boats hung upon a rock, and a hot skirmish with the Cherokees on the mountain side took place before they could extricate her."

Among those who shared the dangers of this voyage was Rachael Donelson, the daughter of the leader, "a black-eyed, 'black-haired brunette, as gay, as bold, and as handsome a lass as ever danced on the deck of a flatboat". She took the helm while her father took a shot at the Indians. She later became the wife of General Andrew Jackson. I guess "he loved her for the dangers she had passed."

Rachel (Donelson) Jackson

The party of Colonel Donelson boldly shot the Muscle Shoals without a pilot. They were the first whites who ever set their eyes on the soil of Lawrence County, Alabama of which we have an account. After a voyage of four months they reached their new home and there was a happy meeting of husbands and wives, parents and children. Thomas Green, along with two sons and Cato West traveled by boat along the Tennessee in 1782.

Another attempt to settle Muscle Shoals was made by Colonel James Robertson in 1787, but he was again forced out.

A pioneer, Zachariah Cox, brought a colony with him and managed to stay in the area for two years before the Indians burned the block house and small village to the ground. He tried one more time but was again driven out.

The Honorable Felix Grundy, a Representative and a Senator from Tennessee, once alluded to the early settlers difficulties in this excerpt from a speech made in the United States

Senate:

To give the reader some idea of the manner in which early settlers were harassed by the Indians, it has been stated that for fifteen years they killed within seven miles of Nashville one person in about every ten days. Then, woman and children were slaughtered indiscriminately, and this ruthless warfare extended to all the settlements in Middle Tennessee.

I was too young to participate in these dangers and difficulties, but I can remember when death was in almost every bush, and every thicket concealed an ambuscade. If I am asked to trace my memory back, and name the first indelible impression it received, it would be the sight of my eldest brother, bleeding and dying under the wounds inflicted by the tomahawk and scalping knife. Another, and another went in the same way. I have seen a widowed mother plundered of her whole property in one night; from affluence and ease reduced to poverty in a moment, and compelled to labor with her own hands to support and educate her last and favorite son-him who now addresses you. Sir, the ancient sufferings of the West were very great. I know it. I need turn to no document to tell me what they were. They are written upon my memory-a part of them on my heart. Those of us who are here are but the remnant, the wreck of large families lost in the settlement of the West.

After a while, the patience of the settlers was completely exhausted by these attacks and they determined to strike a blow which would reach the heart of the enemy at their stronghold, Nickajack, an area generally referred to as the rugged Applachian foothills in eastern Tennessee and northeastern Alabama. From this point the Cherokees, with their allies, were accustomed to making their incursions. Nickajack was their great military station, where the warriors from the Little Tennessee above and the Muscle Shoals below, concentrated. And here, in riotous drunkenness, they consumed the "fruits of their victories."

The whites had never crossed the Tennessee, and the Indians felt secure. General James Robertson collected a force of six hundred men with much secrecy, and burst upon them at Nickajack, like a thunderbolt.

The six hundred men reached the north bank of the river after dark, constructed small rafts for their guns and ammunition, and pushed them before them—sometimes wading and sometimes swimming. They reached the southern bank early in the morning, surrounded their enemies, and gained an overwhelming victory. The power of the tribe was completely broken. The Cherokees for the first time sued for peace, and never afterward molested the whites.

Joseph Martin and John Donelson, acting as agents of William Blount and Richard Caswell, bought the Great Bend area of the Tennessee River from the Indians. In 1783, Griffin, Rutherford, Anthony Bledsoe and John Sevier joined Martin and Donelson in the venture.

William Blount influenced the States of Georgia and North Carolina to create Houston county, to be governed by a commission of seven men that included Martin, Donelson and Sevier. Donelson was surveyor, Sevier was Milita Colonel Commandant and Martin became Indian Agent. Wade Hampton from South Carolina joined the group venture.

In total, eighty men moved into the area of Muscle Shoals and Valentine Sevier was appointed as a member of the Georgia Legislature. However, two weeks after becoming settled in Muscle Shoals, they were forced out by the Native Americans again.

Injured, Robbed And Traveling On Foot, They Still Made It To Alabama In 1791

The Tombigbee river derives its name from a Spaniard, who settled very early on its banks and manufactured trunks and boxes for the Indians. They called him 'Tom Beckabee' which in their language signifies 'Tom the box maker.' The Tombigbee river bounds Greene county on the southwest and west.

The Tombigbee District was one of the first to be colonized by British subjects from the Thirteen Colonies in what was at the time West Florida outside the colonial outpost of Mobile.

White settlers from other states had begun to settle on the lower 'Bikbee' (Tombigbee) around 1790. They came very slowly, however, and numbered only twelve hundred and fifty souls ten years later when a census was taken. The trackless wilderness that lay between was filled with obstacles and perils that none but the boldest dared to encounter. This area in 1800 comprised the first county of the southern part of the Mississippi Territory and was named Washington.

In February 1791, a party of emigrants, consisting of Colonel Thomas Kimbel, John Barnett, Robert Sheffield, Barton Hannon, and Mounger with a wife and children, three of whom were grown, set out from Georgia for the Tombigbee.

Entering the Creek nation, one of the children was injured by a fall, which compelled the elder Mounger and his younger family to stop upon the trail. They were later robbed by the Indians of everything they possessed and had to make their way back to Georgia on foot.

The three young Moungers and the other emigrants continued to the Tensaw, passing the creeks and rivers upon rafts. They found upon their arrival at Tensaw the Halls, Byrnes, Mims, Kilcreas, Steadhams, Easlies, Linders and others.

Crossing the Alabama and Tombigbee upon rafts, they found residing below McIntosh Bluff, the Bates, Lawrences and Powells. Above there, on the Tombigbee, they discovered the Danley, Wheets, Johnsons, McGrews, Hockets, Freelands, Talleys and Bakers.

Among these few people, Colonel Kimbel and his little party established themselves, and began the cultivation of the soil with their horses, upon the backs of which they had brought a few axes and plows.

The garrison at St. Stephens was composed of one company, commanded by Captain Fernando Lisoro. The block house, the residence of the commandant, and the church, were good buildings, of frame-work, clay and plaster. The other houses were small, and covered with cypress bark. All the inhabitants of this place, and of the country, were required to labor so many days upon the public works, to bake the oath of allegiance, and to assist in repelling the depredations of the Creeks, who stole horses and other property.

Some French farmers also lived upon this river. They dwelt in houses made almost entirely of clay while those of the Americans were constructed of small poles in the rudest manner. They all cultivated indigo, which was worth two dollars and fifty cents per pound. The burning of tar engaged much of the time of the Spaniards, still lower down.

Sophia McGillivray,
A Remarkable Woman

"Upon Little river, dividing the modern counties of Baldwin and Monroe, lived many intelligent and wealthy people, whose blood was a mixture of white and Indian. This colony was formed at an early period, for the benefit of their large stocks of cattle, for the wild grass and cane were here never killed by the frost."

The sister of General McGillivray lived among these people. Sophia McGillivray, "a maiden beautiful in all respects," was living upon the Coosa River when Benjamin Durant, a man of Huguenot blood, came from South Carolina to her mother's house. He was a "youth of astonishing strength and activity, who had mastered all who opposed him at home."

Traders told him that a man in the Creek nation "was his superior" so he immediately set out for that region. Durant was handsome and "his complexion was almost as brown as that of the pretty, dark-eyed Sophia."

Sophia went with him to the Hickory Ground, only a few miles distant where many Indians had collected to see him meet the other man. After they met with the warrior, a tremendous fight ensued which Durant won and he was "proclaimed the champion of the nation."

Durant married Sophia and went to reside upon one of the estates of her father, the wealthy Lachlan McGillivray, who was situated upon the Savannah river. During the siege of Savannah, she was there with her father, her husband and her little boy.

Land lying between Montgomery and Selma was cultivated by Benjamin Durant as early as 1786.

Sophia Durant had an air of authority about her, equal, if not superior to that of her brother, Alexander McGillivray.

She was much better acquainted with the Indian tongue, since he had lived far away from the Indian nation for many years. Whenever he held councils in the vicinity of Sophia's residence, she was accustomed to deliver his sentiments in a speech. Her husband became a wealthy man, and 'Durant's Bend' and other places upon the Alabama still preserve his memory.

In the summer of 1790 while her brother was at New York, the Creeks threatened to descend upon the Tensaw settlers and put them to death. Though nine months pregnant, Sophia Durant mounted a, horse, and with a black woman by her side, the two women set out from Little River. They camped out at night and on the fourth day, they arrived at the Hickory Ground. She immediately assembled the Chiefs and threatened them with the vengeance of her brother when he returned if they continued with their plans. The ringleaders were arrested and her actions put a complete stop to their murderous intentions.

Two weeks afterward, this energetic and gifted woman was delivered of twins at the Hickory Ground. One of them married James Bailey who was killed at the fall of Fort Mims, in 1813, and the other lived to be an old woman.

North Carolinians Persevere And Finally Arrive In Alabama

A North Carolina party left their homes on the Atlantic slope in December of 1801. Some of the names were: Thomas Malone and family, James More, Goodway Myrick, George Nosworthy, Robert Caller, and William Murrell. With them were sixty slaves. They crossed the Blue Ridge, and came to the Tennessee. At Knoxville they made flat-boats and reached the head of the Muscle Shoals by floating with the current.

Typical flatboat in 1801 from engraving by Alfred Waud

Packing their household goods on their horses which had come down the river on land, they started for the "Bigbee settlements." They reached the Cotton Gin, a short distance above the present town of Aberdeen where they embarked in some long canoes to continue their journey.

They soon wrecked, and lost all their goods, tools, guns, all their effects—except the clothes upon their persons. One white child and twenty-one slaves were drowned.

From a historian's words we learn the details of their experience:

Desiring to lessen the fatigues of the long and painful trip, the party constructed two canoes at this point, each forty feet in length, and very large, but of miserable workmanship, being executed with no other tools than axes and grubbing hoes. These they placed in the river, in parallel positions, five feet apart. They were connected by a platform made of cane, upon which were deposited the effects of the expedition, which were piled up high above the heads of the emigrants, who now sat down in long rows in the two canoes.

A few of the men went by land with the horses towards St. Stephens, to make preparations for the arrival of the main party. This rude and singular craft, then quite common in savage regions, had proceeded but two miles down the rapid, crooked and swollen stream, when it struck with great force against a log, which extended half across the channel, and immediately disappeared. The cane ligament which bound the Siamese canoes burst asunder, and every soul was washed deep under the waves. Those who rose again were presently seen struggling with the torrent, amid the wreck, now tossed about in the fury of the waters.

Murrel rose, but in his arms was the lifeless body of a daughter. His wife also came to the surface, with a babe at her breast, both, happily, alive. Malone and others, swimming ashore, became active in assisting many of the party in reaching limbs of trees by extending to them grapevines and canes. At length, all who survived huddled upon a small piece of land, surrounded by water.

It was now night. The north wind swept over the gloomy swamp. The ducks, in their rapid flight, whizzed through the air. The wolves howled upon the prairies. The owls screamed and hooted upon the lofty trees. The mighty timber crashed as the angry currents passed by. Such were the unwelcome sounds that fell upon the ears of this

64

miserable party. No succor came. No encouraging voice saluted them. Benumbed with cold, they hovered together to keep alive, shivering and knocking their agitated limbs against each other, while their wet apparel froze fast upon them.

Being without fire, they had no way to produce one. It was two miles back to the old camp, and the route lay over thick cane, water and small islands. A resolute young negro man volunteered to find it. He plunged into the low grounds, and, strangely, made his way to the camp. In the meantime, the helpless pioneers, despairing of his return, bewailed their condition with deep moans and bitter lamentations. Beneath the shadows of one of the darkest nights ever known, they mournfully counted over the missing and the drowned.

Two long hours passed away, when the cheerful halloo of the negro was heard afar off. It was answered by a united and sympathetic shout. All eyes were turned in the direction from which the sound came, and in the darkness was seen an indistinct light, which shone over the tops of the distant canes like a far-off Aurora Borealis. It was fire, and the noble negro had brought it from the old camp. At length he came, with a cracking, crashing noise, familiar only to the ears of those who have walked through the dense cane swamps of Alabama.

Fires were kindled with dry cane, and around them sat the sufferers until the morning sun dispelled the horrid night. It was now ascertained that one white child and twenty-one black servants were entombed beneath the tide of the angry Tombigbee. The survivors groped their way to the Cotton Gin, without provisions, without hats, without tools, without firearms, without money, and with no clothes except those which drooped upon their limbs They were friendless and alone in a savage country, far from their point of destination, and still further from their native land.

They continued to press on and and after a journey, from North Carolina of one hundred and twenty days, they finally reached their destination. They were saved from starvation by their faithful hunting dogs. The dogs procured for them rabbits, raccoon, and opossums.

The first named of this party of settlers, Thomas Malone, was then a young man. He had been a clerk in the high office at Raleigh, and became afterward clerk of the court of Washington county.

Milly, Alone In The Wilderness Of Montgomery, Alabama In 1792

The territory of the present county of Montgomery contained only a few white inhabitants in 1792. Among these, there was a white woman, who had lived with her husband at Savannah. He was a foot soldier in one of the British regiments, but deserted from the army. He and his wife fled to the Chattahoochie River area to avoid the automatic death penalty for treason to the British Crown in time of war. He died at Cusseta.

Milly, his "bold and adventurous wife continued to wander through the Creek nation after his death." The Creeks thought Milly was an enchanted, 'Medicine Woman'. She finally settled in the territory of the present county of Montgomery near what is now Waugh and Mt. Meigs. She lived on the eastern side of a creek, which still bears her name, for she was called by no other than that of "Milly." (Also called the Narcoce Chappo).

She established herself among the Cuwalla Indians, alone, without husband, father, children, or even a single friend. "Espousing one of the sons of the forest, she soon began to have comforts around her. Her stock of cattle became large, to which was added in a few years, a large drove of ponies." She built a rugged home, tavern and a toll bridge. Soon she developed a thriving business.

Milly lived alone upon this creek for many years. The trading path leading from Pensacola to Tookabatcha passed by her house and in 1792, "her solitary hours were agreeably relieved by the prattle of a little white girl."

A party of Creeks advanced to the Georgia frontiers around 1790 and attacked some whites. They surrounded the house of a family named Scarlett, killed him and his wife and children. A child of a neighbor, Tempey Ellis was a little girl about eight years old at the time and was in the house when the attack was occurred. She concealed herself under the bed.

A warrior discovered Tempey Ellis and dragged her out by the hair and raised his hatchet to kill her, but decided he could possibly obtain a handsome sum for her ransom so he placed the child on his horse and carried her to Auttose on the Tallapoosa. She was often beaten and made to bring water from the springs.

Milly heard that the Auttoses had a white girl in slavery and she set out mounted her pony immediately and rode to Auttose. She paid ten ponies and six head of cattle for Tempey and the next day carried this unfortunate child to her house. "For several years she acted the part of a most affectionate mother. Subsequently the child was delivered to Seagrove, the Creek Agent, at St. Mary's, and was sent from thence to her friends in Georgia."

Old Milly was exceedingly attached to Tempey and gave her up with great reluctance. Tempey Ellis grew up to become a respectable old woman, the wife of Mr. Thomas Frizell and resided in Pike county, Alabama.

It is believed that she latter married a Jesse Evans because the old tavern's name was later changed to Evans Tavern.

When Vice-President Aaron Burr was arrested in Alabama, Burr, along with a number of his guards visited Milly's Tavern and her husband was said to have conducted the party across the rain swollen creeks.

Montgomery County, Alabama
Inhabited By Some Interesting Characters

The area of present day Montgomery county, Alabama was once a wilderness inhabited by Indians and the few interesting characters in the early days of the future state of Alabama.

William Gregory

Within a few miles of 'Milly of Montgomery' lived William Gregory. He had resided for years among the Indians and became a stock-keeper. He lived in a cabin with his Indian family. His beautiful and gently rolling land stretched as far as the eye could see. He had cattle and horses and was undisturbed by man or beast.

"It was said that William Gregory was a kind-hearted man, who fed the wanderer "without money and without price," and who, even in a lawless land, possessed a heart which prompted him to be honest."

Abram Mordecai Marker

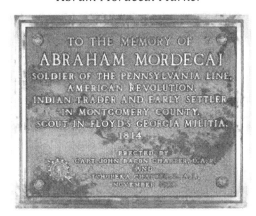

Abram Mordecai

In 1785, Abram Mordecai, a Jew from Pennsylvania, arrived in the area and established a trading house at the two miles west of Line

Creek.

Abram Mordecai dwelt fifty years in the Creek nation and set up the first commercial cotton gin at Coosada Bluff near Montgomery. It was his belief that the Native Americans were originally of his people. He asserted that in their 'Green Corn Dances' he'd heard them utter in grateful tones the word yavoyaha! yavoyuho! He was always informed by the Indians that this meant Jehovah, or the Great Spirit, and that they were then returning thanks for the abundant harvest with which they were blessed.

Albert Pickett described him in the following anecdote:

> Abram Mordecai, an Indian trader, procuring the consent of the Creek Chiefs and the approbation of Col. Hawkins, had established a cotton gin at Weatherford's race track, on the first eastern bluff below the junction of the Coosa and Tallapoosa. It was built by Lyons & Barnett, of Georgia, who brought their tools, gin saws and other materials from that State on pack-horses.
>
> He traded extensively with the Indians, exchanging his goods for pink root, hickory-nut oil and peltries of all kinds. These he carried to New Orleans and Mobile in boats, and to Pensacola and Augusta on pack-horses. The hickory-nut oil was a luxury with French and Spanish epicures. It was manufactured by the Indians in a simple manner--by boiling the cracked nuts in water, and skimming off the oil as it floated on the surface.
>
> Mordecai bought cotton of the Indians in small quantities, ginned it, and carried it to Augusta on pack-horses in bags. He was a dark-eyed Jew, and amorous in his disposition. Tourculla, (Captain Isaacs,) the Chief of the Coosawdas, hearing of his intrigues with a married squaw, approached his house with twelve warriors, knocked him down, thrashed him with poles until he lay insensible, cut off his ear, and left him to the care of his wife. They also broke up his boat, and burned down his gin-house. A pretty squaw

was the cause of the destruction of the first cotton gin in Alabama.

James Russell

Another trader James Russell, a Tory, also lived in the vicinity. He came to the area in order to be rid of Whig persecution.

Other up-country traders, were

- Woccocoie Clarke who lived at Woccocoie, in the modern Coosa county. He transported his merchandise and skins upon seventy pack-horses. His wife was an Indian maiden who was of great assistance to him. She was called Queen Anne for the Queen of England. Clarke was an Englishman.

- A Tory named Love, and Dargan a Dutchman and a notorious horse thief lived near the site of Mount Meigs. There they carried on a small commerce.

- At Econchate, Red Ground, which embraces the southern suburbs of the city of Montgomery, lived several white traders.

- Charles Weatherford established a trading house upon the first eastern bluff below the confluence of the Coosa and Tallapoosa where he laid out the first race-paths ever known in East Alabama. "Often would the noted horse thief, fresh from the frontiers of Georgia, here for the first time try the speed of his stolen ponies."

- "The most blood-thirsty, fiendish and cruel white man that ever inhabited any country was Savannah Jack, or, as be was universally called by this outlawed world, 1792 "Savaner Jack". He lived at Souvanoga, upon the Tallapoosa and boasted that "he had killed so many women and children, upon the Cumberland and Georgia frontiers in company with his town's people that he could swim in their blood if it was collected in one pool."

All over the territory of Alabama and Mississippi, wherever an Indian town of importance was found, white traders lived. Some of them became wealthy, but like all property acquired in a commerce with Indians, it generally left the owner in his old age.

Living With The Native Americans

Some Of The Alabama Pioneers Captured And Ransomed By The Native Americans

In 1792, there were no white settlements between the Alabama river and northward in the vicinity of Nashville and the Creeks often attacked white settlers to drive them out. They pushed their hostilities to the very doors of Nashville.

The house of Thompson, a wealthy and respectable man, was attacked and the whole family except for a daughter was killed. She was taken into captivity to Kialigee, upon the Tallapoosa river along with an amiable lady, named Caffrey and her little son. When they arrived in Kialigeen, the prisoners found another woman, Sarah Fletcher, who was captured years before in the Miro district, which was also called Cumberland district.

"Miss Thompson was ransomed by Riley, a trader, for eight hundred weight of dressed deer-skins, worth two hundred and sixty dollars, and was treated with kindness by her benefactor, and restored to her friends."

However, Mrs. Caffrey was separated from her son, beaten with sticks, scratched with gar's teeth, and made to work in the fields. Two years went by and then she was carried to Nashville where she was ransomed.

Her son, having been separated from her at an early age, became Indian in his feelings. It took five years and considerable difficulty before Abram Mordecai was able to separate him from his Native American playmates and carry him to Seagrove. Mordecai sent him to Governor Blount and he was eventually reunited with his mother.

The Coosawdas, who lived upon the Alabama, were frequently out upon the Cumberland, engaged in the massacre of the settlers and the plunder of their effects. Captain Isaacs, the Chief, returned in 1792 with Elizabeth Baker, a young lady from Cumberland. "How miserable and lonely must have been the journey, with these sanguinary warriors. who bore the scalps of her father, mother, brothers and sisters, daily suspended upon poles before her eyes."

She found a friend in Charles Weatherford, who lived across the river. He ransomed Miss Baker, and placed her in charge of his wife, Sehoy, the half sister of General McGillivray and the mother of the celebrated William Weatherford. She ultimately reached her friends.

A white woman named Mrs. Crawley was captured in Tennessee and taken to the Black Warrior village. Tandy Walker went on foot to visit his friend, Oce-Oche-Motla, and secretly obtained a canoe. He then slipped off with Mrs. Crawley at night and carried her to St. Stephens. "She was sick, and crazed from suffering and anxiety." Ann, Mr. Gaines wife, nursed her back to health. Then Colonel Haynes and Thomas Malone bought a horse, bridle, and saddle and sent her with a party of gentlemen back to her home at the mouth of the Tennessee and Tandy Walker became a hero in his hometown.

Surveying Alabama
Trading Houses Established

In 1797 a ferry was established by Samuel Mims across the Alabama and another by Hollinger, an old resident among the Indians, across the Tombigbee. The route of travel crossed the Island called Nannahubba below the cut-off.

A change for the settlers under Spanish rule was near at hand. Arrangements were made by the United States Government to have the line of latitute 31° established. The line defines the part of the border between the states of Mississippi and Louisiana, and most of the border between Alabama and Florida.

In 1797 Colonel Andrew Elliott, one of the commissioners to mark this boundary line between Spanish and United States territory, marched his troops and corps of wood-men and surveyors to a dense swamp on the east of the Mississippi where it was ascertained that the line left the river. He was soon joined by Major Minor and Sir William Dunbar, Spanish commissioners. Spain also furnished troops.

The advance along the line resembled the movement of an army. The trees were blazed along the line, and mounds of earth thrown up at the end of each mile.

The surveyors overcame the difficulties in crossing the rivers and swamps, and passed beyond the Tensaw. Passing through the Creek lands the party met with obstacles and opposition from the Indians, and also from the Spaniards. They marked the line only as far as the Chattahoochie, but the surveyors passed across to the St. Mary's and by February of 1800 established the point on that river of the line of 31° in the presence of Colonel Elliott and Major Minor. The spot was marked by a a large earth mound. The United States now had a recognized southern boundary line.

In 1801 a treaty was made with the Choctaws, to obtain a tract of land extending some distance north from St. Stephens. The Choctaws claimed east of the Tombigbee to the water-shed or dividing ridge.

The Creeks did not acknowledge their rights, and at the treaty in 1802 one of their chiefs by the name of Mad Wolf is reported to have said, "the people of Tombigbee have put over their cattle in the fork, on the Alabama hunting grounds and have gone a great way on our lands. I want them put back. We all know they are Americans." From this speech it is evident that at this time there were whites occupying lands east of the Tombeckbee.

St. Stephens Marker

In the same year a trading house was established at St. Stephens, designed especially for the Choctaw Indians. This establishment was called a factory. Joseph Chambers was appointed Superintendent and Thomas H. Williams, both from North Carolina, assistant. The latter became afterward secretary of the territory, collector of the port of New Orleans, and United States senator from Mississippi. George S. Gaines of Virginia, then residing in Tennessee, was afterward appointed assistant, and came to St. Stephens in the spring of 1805.

At that time "the parsonage of the old Spanish church was used as a skin-house," the block house was used for a government store room. In 1807, Gaines became what was called principal factor, having an assistant, a 'skin-man' or fur and hide tender, and an interpreter.

The job of the tender was to examine the furs and hides carefully during the summer, sort them, and in the fall pack them in bales for shipment to Philadelphia. The articles brought for sale or exchange by the Choctaws were furs and peltries of various kinds, bears' oil, honey, beeswax, bacon, tobacco, and ground peas. In 1809, they amounted in value to more than seven thousand dollars.

To avoid the payment of Spanish duties at Mobile, the Government arranged a line for conveying goods to the warehouse and trading post down the Ohio river and up the Tennessee to a point called Colbert's Ferry. They then were packed on horses and carried along a horse path through the Chickasaws to Peachland's upon the Tombeigbee where the goods were transported by boats to St. Stephens.

In October 1802 the Pierce brothers established a cotton gin at the boat yard in this region and started merchandising. This gin was built by the same contractors, Lyons and Barnett, who also built the first one at McIntosh's Bluff on the Tombigbee. It was the third cotton gin for these river settlements.

Mississippi Territory Created
Governor Blount Ousted
First School Opened

In 1798, the Congress of the United States created the Mississippi Territory in the region between 31º and 32º 28' of north latitude, with the Mississippi river for the western and the Chattahoochee for the eastern boundary. President Adams appointed Winthrop Sargent of Massachusetts the governor of this area.

Congress included a part of West Florida in April of 1798 as a part of the Mississippi Territory. This territory was described as, "on the west by the Mississippi river, on the north by a line drawn due east from the mouth of the Yazoo to the Chattahoochie, and on the south by the thirty-first degree of north latitude."

Governor Winthrop Sargent

Governor Sargent assumed authority of the Mississippi Territory and Natchez became the seat of government. The first public building was a jail built at Natchez. Territorial Judges were Peter Bruin and William McGuire.

On the second of April 1799, Governor Winthrop Sargent issued a proclamation dividing the Territory into two counties, the northern to be called Adams and the southern Pickering.

Lieutenant McLeary took possession of Fort St. Stephens on the May 5, 1799. The Spanish garrison marched out and descended the river below the recently surveyed line of latitude 31°.

In July of the same year, Fort Stoddert was established, about six miles above the Spanish boundary and three miles below the commencement of Mobile river. A stockade was built there with one bastion.

Mobile River looking north from site of Fort Stoddert

Among the inhabitants on Lake Tensaw, at the boat yard, were the two brothers, John and William Pierce from New England. They had settled in the area when the Spanish owned the area. William followed weaving, which was a very profitable skill in those days. John Pierce opened a school, believed to be the first American school in Alabama.

The historian Albert Pickett states: "There the high-blood descendants of Lachlan McGillivray, the Taits, Weatherfords, and Durants, the aristocratic Linders, the wealthy Mim's, and the children of many others, first learned to read. The pupils were strangely mixed in blood and their color was of every hue."

In May 1799, a detachment of federal troops relieved the Spanish garrison at Fort St. Stephens. In the south, Fort Stoddert was erected in July below the junction of the Alabama and Tombigbee.

Pickering and Adams Counties were the Northern part of the territory and bordered what was to later become Madison County, Alabama. The first Sheriff of Pickering County was Lewis Evans while William Ferguson was the Sheriff of Adams. Henry Hunter, James Hoggett, Anthony Hutchins and Sutton Banks were freshman legislators from the Adams County to the house of representatives or general assembly as it was first called. Cato West, Thomas M. Green, John Burnett and Thomas Calvit were from Pickering County and John F. McGrew was from Washington County though he was not seated.

By proclamation, in June 1800, Governor Sargent established Washington county, the limits of which comprised all of the territory east of Pearl River as far as the Chattahoochee and this became the first county in the future Alabama. The same year congress provided for a legislature for the Territory.

The first census of Washington county took place in 1800 and it was found that "733 whites 494 negro slaves and 23 free negroes were living in the area." The population of Mobile and Baldwin, not then existing as counties, but under Spanish rule, was probably as large.

Many settlers resented the arbitrary conduct of Governor Sargent and they sent up a petition for his removal so in 1801, President Jefferson commissioned William C. C. Claiborne of Tennessee to succeed him.

The new governor, a native of Virginia, possessed much ability. He removed the capital of the Territory to Washington, a village six miles east of Natchez.

On April 24, 1802, "the State of Georgia ceded to the federal government all the territory embraced within the limits of the present States of Alabama and Mississippi, north of the parallel 31°, for the sum of $1,250,000. The commissioners on the part of the federal government who concluded this purchase were Messrs. James Madison of Virginia, Albert Gallatin of Pennsylvania, and Levi Lincoln of Massachusetts; on the part of Georgia, Messrs. James Jackson, Abraham Baldwin, and John Milledge of that State. Thus, after a vexations controversy, the claim made by that State to this extensive realm was extinguished."

In 1802, Claiborne became a county of the Mississippi Territory. Settlement of the new Territory continued slowly for the first few years because the hazards of penetrating the pathless wilderness which lay between it and the states were augmented by the presence of inhospitable Indians.

Immigration was also retarded due to the difficulty of getting the produce of the country to market. There were export duties to be paid at Fort Stoddert to the United States, and a tariff at Mobile to be paid to Spain. The character of the population in the Mississippi Territory was originally of the rudest kind. Schools and churches were still basically unknown.

The boundaries of the Mississippi Territory extended northward to the Tennessee line, whereby it was almost trebled in size. But the Indian title remained to all of its area, save to a slip of country above and below Natchez, and the one on the Tombigbee. A second treaty was made in October 17, 1802, between the federal government and the Choctas, (Choctaws) at Fort Confederation, on the Tombigbee. "It related principally to the cession made to the British, and was signed by Brig. Gen. James Wilkinson of the federal army, on the part of the government, by Okechummee and Tuskamayabee on the part of the northern district, by Tuskana Hopoyo, Mingo Pooskoos, and Pushmataha on the part of the south-eastern district, and by Mingo Homastubbee, Tuskahoma, Latallahoma, and Mooklahoosapoyee on the part of the western district, of the tribe."

By a supplementary act in 1804, there was annexed to this Territory all the 'tract of country' south of the state of Tennessee bounded on the east by the state of Georgia and on the west by Louisiana.

Robert Williams of North Carolina succeeded Governor Claiborne in 1805.

Around this time, William Blount, an early pioneer of Alabama, was ousted from the United States Senate, for conspiring with the British.

They Made Sure The Knot
Was Tied Securely

On the 4th of June 1800, Governor Sargent called into existence by proclamation the county of Washington. Settlements in the area of Washington County were according to the American state papers, as quoted by Meek, "thinly scattered along the western banks of the Mobile and Tombigby, (Tombigbee) for more than seventy miles, and extending nearly seventy-five miles upon the eastern borders of the Mobile and Alabama."

The two main settlements of whites were upon land which the Indian occupants had formerly ceded to the British or Spanish authorities. Here the inhabitants were living without any civil government over them at the time. They had no magistrates, no ministers, and no marriage ceremonies. Young people were accustomed to pairing off and living together as husbands and wives with the promise to be married whenever a minister or magistrate arrived.

Washington was probably the largest county in the Mississippi Territory, those of Adams and Pickering excepted, that had then been called into existence by executive or legislative power. Its boundaries were the same as those of the territory on the north, east, and south, or latitude 32°28', the Chattahoochie, and the thirty-first parallel; and the Pearl river on the west. Most of that vast region was then occupied by Indian tribes, over which tribes the Government had no control.

A humorous instance was recorded of a couple who wished to be bound together in a more traditional setting than the simple pairing off.

Daniel Johnson and Miss Elizabeth Linder of Lake Tensaw were in love. However, he was poor and she an heiress so her parents objected to them being wed. On Christmas night of 1800, a large party was assembled at the house of Samuel Mims and among them were the two lovers.

While everyone was enjoying the music, the dance, and Christmas festivities, a few young people accompanied Daniel Johnson and Elizabeth Linder as they secretly left the house. The party embarked on board some canoes, paddled down the lake, and into the Alabama River. They arrived at Fort Stoddert an hour before the dawn of the next day.

Captain Shaumburg, a cheerful German, in command of the fort was called upon to perform the marriage ceremony. In vain, he declared his ignorance of such ceremonies and his want of authority. He was told that he was placed there by the federal government to protect the people and regulate their affairs, and that this little affair needed his sanctioned.

At length the captain yielded to their solicitations, and having the two lovers placed before him proclaimed: "I Captain Shaumburg, of the 2nd regiment of the United States army, and commandant of Fort Stoddert, do hereby pronounce you man and wife. Go home! behave yourselves; multiply, and replenish the Tensaw country!"

They reentered their canoes, returned to the Tensaw boat yard, and the whole settlement pronounced them to be "the best married people they had known in a long time." Justices of the peace later arrived in the settlement as well as courts and judges, and also in a few years ministers of the Gospel.

A Unique Native American Way To Settle
A Land Dispute

In 1805, only an Indian trail led from the distant Oconee river to Lake Tensaw. This wide extent of country was held by the Muscogee or Creek Indians. The Georgia colony did not seem to have extended their settlements west of the Oconee river, and after the Revolution in 1783 and 1786 the state of Georgia vainly endeavored by treaties to obtain peaceable possession of the lands east of a line extending from the union of the Ockmulgee and Oconee to the St. Mary's river, including the islands and harbors of that southern coast.

Peaceable possession of these lands was not obtained until the treaty was made by President Washington at New York with Colonel McGillivray in 1790. West of the line named and of the Oconee river the Creek nation held possession.

In the fall of 1805, thirty Creek chiefs and warriors, a delegation from their nation, went to Washington D. C. While they were there, the general government obtained from them the right "of using a horse path through their country," the chiefs agreed to build bridges, or have ferries cross the streams, and to open houses of entertainment for travelers. A route of travel was thus finally secured for emigrants from Georgia into the wilds between the rivers.

At the same time, the Choctaw Indians ceded to the United States five million acres of their lands, beginning at the 'Cut Off', (southern limit of Clarke county), half way between the two rivers, running north along the water shed, to the Choctaw corner, which was later the northern boundary of Clarke county and thence on or near the second range line east, then west to the Fulluctabuna old fields, or to the mouth of Fluctabuna Creek, then crossing the Tombigbee, west to the Mississippi settlements, south to latitude 31° called Elliott's line, and east to the Mobile river, and north to the 'Cut Off'.

Thus a grant of land was obtained lying east of the Tombigbee river where those pioneers, coming through the Creek nation, might settle and make homes without intruding upon Indian rights. Other claimants soon appeared for the strip of territory east of the Tombigbee and extending half way to the Alabama.

However, a dispute ensued when the Creek Indians claimed that this land belonged to them rather than to the Choctaws, and that the Choctaws had no right to cede to the United States any lands east of the Tombigbee.

Instead of resorting to arms or to diplomacy the Creeks agreed to risk their claims on the success of a game of ball. Old settlers in Clarke County, Alabama referred to this game as a fact well authenticated and attested by eyewitnesses. John Scarborough, who was eighty-five years of age in 1882 was one of those who witnessed it.

The contestants in the game laid aside most of their clothing. The Creeks were described as having been "slim and straight in person," while the Choctaws as shorter, but "active as cats." It was said that the first game was played by warriors against warriors, and that the Choctaws won, but the Creeks were dissatisfied.

"The Choctaws offered to let their squaws play against the Creek squaws. The offer was accepted and the women played. Again the Choctaws won. The Creeks therefore gave up their claims. According to early settlers, the game took place at an old play-ground near the old site of Elam church, near the corner-post that was finally driven in the ground. The post marked the boundary between Choctaw and Creek."

"For the last time, after the decisive game between the Indian women, this strip came into the possession of those who proposed to hold it against Creeks or any other claimants or invaders."

In 1808 the line was surveyed from Hal's Lake to the Choctaw corner. Previous to this time, in the disputed region, the Choctaws and Creeks had both hunted and fought for the game. While the surveyors were on the the ground, the Indians agreed to a line that should cross no water.

One who traveled in various directions across this disputed territory would suppose such a line very difficult to be traced. It is said that twenty chiefs of each party went along with their tomahawks to blaze the trees.

The whole space between the Alabama and Tombigbee and further north extended even to the mouth of the Black Warrior, had been ceded by the Choctaws to the British in a treaty made at Mobile, March 26, 1765.

In the early days of the Mississippi Territory, Natchez, or the new town of Washington a few miles east, was quite a distance from St. Stephens and inconvenient for the adequate administration of justice.

Congress made the Tombigbee region a revenue district, calling it the district of Mobile. At Fort Stoddert duties were exacted upon merchandise brought in and also required upon products sent out. These duties, and additional duties exacted by the Spaniards at Mobile bore heavily upon the settlers. As one illustration, in the year 1807 the Natchez planters in the western part of the territory paid four dollars a barrel for Kentucky flour and the same flour cost the Tombeigbee planters sixteen dollars.

After many complaints from the citizenry, the president of the United States authorized that a supreme court judge should be appointed for the settlers along the Tombigbee River.

Hon. Harry Toulmin, born in England, sought religious freedom in America. He was president of Transylvania University at Lexington for four years, and secretary of state of Kentucky for eight years, a good scholar, fine writer, and well versed in law. He was selected for the new position.

At first he settled near Fort Stoddert, then removed to the court house and named it Wakefield. He held his first court there in 1804 or 1805. At this time there were some seven or eight hundred inhabitants on the Tensaw and the Alabama rivers, and in the fork, besides those on the western side of the Tombigbee. Wakefield is where Vice President Aaron Burr was arrested.

The next year Thomas Bassett, Edward Creighton, James Denby, Sr. and George Brewer, Jr. were appointed commissioners for the town of Wakefield some twenty miles south of St. Stephens. In the fall of 1804, Captain Shaumberg retired from the command, and was succeeded by Captain Schuyler of New York. He was in charge of eighty men. Edmund P. Gaines, was lieutenant, and Lieutenant Reuben Chamberlain was paymaster.

Civilization Arrives

Religion, Patriotism, Laws
And
Civilization

Lorenzo Dow, from Georgia, was recorded as the first prostestant minister in the wilderness area of the Tensaw Boat Yard and Tombigbee area n 1803.

Lorenzo Dow (Library of Congress)

Before this appearance, many of the settlers who were born and bred in the wilderness of Alabama had never even seen a preacher. It was said that one day, he suddenly appeared at the Tensaw Boat Yard. There he proclaimed the "truths of the gospel to a large audience, crossed over the Alabama, and preached two sermons to the 'Bigby settlers' and went from thence to the Natchez

95

settlements, where he also "exhorted the people to turn from the error of their ways."

Rev. Tobias Gibson, a Methodist missionary from South Carolina appears to have visited the Natchez settlements, by way of Cumberland and Ohio in the summer of 1799. He organized religious societies in Washington and its vicinity, and then departed. In the fall of 1800, he was in the Tennessee Conference, and formed about two hundred church members into societies from Bayou Pierre to the Spanish line. He died three years later.

Another Methodist missionary, Rev. Brown came from Tennessee around 1802 to the Natchez settlement. He labored there until 1807. Two Presbyterian ministers also preached in Natchez a few years. From the Baptists, came Rev. David Cooper in 1802 and Dr. Cloud was of the Episcopal church.

The first county court was held at McIntosh Bluff, where John Caller, Cornelius Rain and John Johnson, presided with great frontier dignity. These justices had no code before them, and coming from different States, decided cases according to the laws of their native land. so that the most amusing differences of opinion often prevailed. Laws were adopted and approved for the Mississippi Territory on the tenth of February 1807.

One of the new laws regulated the marriage ceremony. It specified that "any ordained minister must first produce to the orphans court of some county in the territory credentials of his ordination, and of his living in regular communion with his society, and obtain from that court a testimonial authorizing him to solemnize marriage, that testimonial to be granted at the discretion of the court. Pastors however of any society might join together in marriage members of their own society according to their own regulations."

The hour of opening and closing elections in the Mississippi Territory was fixed to take effect after 1808: "That the sheriffs shall open the elections "at twelve of the clock in the forenoon; and shall close at the hour of two in the afternoon, on the subsequent day."

A strict law against bribery had previously been adopted, providing that any representative elected in the Mississippi Territory who should "directly or indirectly give, or agree to give, to any elector, money, meat, drink, or other reward, in order to be elected, or for having been elected, for nay county, shall be expelled, and forever after disabled from holding any office of profit or trust under the government."

The subject of education was not neglected, and Jefferson College had been established at Ellicott's Spring, in the vicinity of the town of Washington.

A partial description of Fort St. Stephens is given by a law enacted in 1807 for laying out a town in Washington County near Fort St. Stephens. "The streets were to be not less than one hundred feet wide on the lands of Edwin Lewis, John Baker, James Morgan and John F. McGrew. These men were also appointed commissioners to lay out the town."

According to Historian Brewer, St. Stephens was first settled by the Spaniards who built a fort about 1786. He did not recognize the prior French occupancy. St. Stephens was laid off into town lots in 1807, and a road was cut to Natchez. An act was also passed to incorporate the Mississippi Society for the acquirement and dissemination of useful knowledge and for the establishment of Jefferson College. Natchez was incorporated and made a city.

Harry Toulmin, James Caller and Lemuel Henry, were appointed to locate and open a road from Natchez to Fort Stoddert. Settlements increased and civilization was advancing.

The cultivation of cotton was rapidly taking the place of the older product indigo. The raising of indigo on the old Spanish and British plantations were abandoned. "The inhabitants of this wilderness were now becoming strongly, in feeling and action, Americans; for in this year of 1807, after the attack by the British on the American vessel the Chesapeake, James McGoffin, already a resident here, having drafted some patriotic resolutions, the inhabitants, "both whigs and tories, participated in an animated public meeting at

Wakefield, pledging their support to the United States, to avenge" this outrage."

However, in 1810, the patriotism of these river settlements in southern part of the Mississippi Territory took a new direction. Due to the presence of the Spaniards still residing below them in the area, they had suffered many annoyances. An expedition was planned for driving the Spaniards out of Mobile.

Troops were raised, boats were loaded with provisions, and the volunteer soldiers passed from the Tensaw Boat Yard down the Tensaw River. But the expedition was not well managed and unsuccessful so the settlers returned home and left the final expulsion of the spaniards to the general government.

Many improvements, in the way of houses, farms and new towns, gave the territory an air of civilization.

The Federal Road
Alabama's First Interstate

After the Louisiana Purchase from France in 1803, the United States government realized a way was needed for settlers and troops to access the new areas. When West Florida was annexed from Spain in 1810, this added to the need for a road.

"The Old Federal Road successfully connected Fort Stoddert to the Chattahoochee River. At that point, the Federal Road merged with the earlier postal riders' horse path that linked Athens, Georgia, to New Orleans, Louisiana. Unlike the old horse path, the Federal Road went eastward making a connection with lands ripe for the recruitment of soldiers and obtaining supplies for the military. This path quickly became a major travel route for pioneers to the area once known as the "Old Southwest."

From its start as a narrow horse path, the Federal Road was used to carry the mails. The Federal Road underwent great development and became a major military road connecting early American forts in the Creek Lands and the Mississippi Territory.

Acting as the interstate highway of its day, when "Alabama Fever" raged through the Carolinas and Georgia, the old Federal Road carried thousands of pioneers to the Southwest. As such, the Federal Road directly contributed to the dramatic increase in Alabama's population between 1810 and 1820—with Alabama's population growing far faster than that of either Mississippi or Louisiana during this time. Alabama continued out-distancing both Mississippi and Louisiana in population growth through 1850.

As the Creek Nation realized that people were doing more than just passing through, and many were settling in their lands, they became increasingly hostile and in 1813-1814 the Creek War began as an attempt to drive the settlers out. The Creek War is also considered by some people to be a continuation of the War of 1812 with Great Britain since the Creeks fought with the British against the United

States during that war.

In August of 1814, the Treaty of Fort Jackson was signed with the Creek Nation which ceded nearly half of Alabama to the United States.

Streets Paved
With
Brick And Stone

In 1807, once lots were laid off near and around the old Fort Stephens, the town of St. Stephens grew rapidly. After the close of the war of 1812, many wealthy people bought lots and erected residences while others settled around in the country. Speculators invested large sums of money in the area, and trades, professions and industries of all kinds soon arrived.

A theater flourished, balls were frequent, however remarkably, there was a prevailing indifference to anything connected with religion. There was not a church building, nor even a church organization in the town for miles around in the early days nor was there provisions made for regular religious services of any kind.

"On rare occasions a minister would make an appointment in the town and preach, but always in a schoolroom or in some private residence that might be courteously tendered him for the occasion. They were usually either Methodist or Baptist preachers. Two ministers did later serve the area of St. Stephens, Reverend Linson of the Methodist faith and Rev. Williams Shoemaker of the Baptist."

The majority of the houses were of brick or rock quarried from the hills nearby in blocks smooth and white as marble. Foundations were laid and cellars were walled up of the same durable materials. Several of the houses were furnished off with a half story and dormer windows. "The customary hall through the center—a necessary feature in a southern climate—was absent. Many of the business houses had rooms in the rear and above the stores for family use."

Streets were paved with brick and stone. "Coming up from the river about a half-mile from the landing a street turned to the north and formed the principal thoroughfare of the town....In 1857 this street was still open, marked by the ruins of houses and shaded by the old china trees."

Around 1812, George Strother Gaines married Ann Gaines, the daughter of Young Gaines from St. Stephens. "His brother, General Edmund Pendleton Gaines, was thrice married, first to Frances the daughter of Judge Harry Toulmin; second to Barbara Blount, the daughter of Governor William Blount of Tennessee; and last to Mrs. Myra Clark Whitney whose long lawsuits for property in New Orleans was known in history."

Some Early Towns In Alabama

Mobile, Mobile County, Alabama

Though, not a part of the United States until 1813, Mobile began as the first capital of colonial French Louisiana in 1702. During its first 100 years, Mobile was a colony of France, then Britain, and lastly Spain. Mobile first became a part of the United States of America in 1813, with the annexation of West Florida under President James Madison.

Government Street, Mobile, Alabama ca. 1900 (Library of Congress)

The European settlement of Mobile, then known as Fort Louis de la Louisiane, started in 1702, at Twenty-seven Mile Bluff on the Mobile River. It was founded by French Canadian brothers Pierre Le Moyne d'Iberville and Jean-Baptiste Le Moyne, Sieur de Bienville, to establish control over France's Louisiana claims.

By the time Mobile was included in the Mississippi Territory in 1813, the population had dwindled to roughly 300 people. The city was included in the Alabama Territory in 1817, after Mississippi gained statehood. Alabama was granted statehood in 1819; Mobile's population had increased to 809 by that time.

Mobile is the county seat of Mobile County, Alabama and as of the 2010 census, the population is 195, 111.

Old St. Stephens, Washington County, Alabama

Americans who took possession of St. Stephens upon the evacuation of Fort Saint Stephens by the Spaniards in 1799. In 1807 lots were laid off near and around the old fort, and a town commenced, which grew rapidly after the close of the war of 1812-15. Many wealthy people bought lots and erected residences; others settled around in the country. Large sums of money were invested; and in trades, professions and industries of all kinds it soon became the peer of any new city of the time.

Old St. Stephens boat dock (Library of Congress)

When the first state assembly adjourned at St. Stephens on February 14, 1818, many Alabama residents thought the capital should be moved to a more central location. Tuscaloosa was under consideration when Governor William Wyatt Bibb made the announcement in 1819 that the capital would be moved to Cahaba. This spelled certain doom for St. Stephens. In addition, the development of shallow draft boats permitted travelers to pass over the shoals and venture further upriver past the town. Lastly, yellow fever outbreaks decimated the citizenry.

By 1833 the old town site was reduced in population to a small village; by the time of the Civil War, it had largely been replaced by the new town.

The Old St. Stephens site lies directly on the river and is no longer inhabited. New St. Stephens developed two miles inland around a railway station, but adjacent to the old site. It is the location of the post office, Baptist and Methodist churches, and residences. There were 495 people residing in New St. Stephens according to the 2010 census.

Huntsville, Madison County, Alabama

In 1811, Huntsville became the first incorporated town in the part of the Mississippi Territory that would soon be in the state of Alabama.

However, the recognized birth year of the city is 1805, the year of John Hunt's arrival. The city's sesquicentennial anniversary was held in 1955, and the bicentennial was celebrated in 2005.

Revolutionary War veteran John Hunt arrived and settled on the land around the Big Spring in 1805. The 1805 Treaty with the Chickasaws and the Cherokee Treaty of Washington of 1806 ceded native claims to the United States Government and the area was subsequently purchased by LeRoy Pope, who named the area Twickenham after the home village of his distant kinsman Alexander Pope.

Due to anti-British sentiment around this time, the name of the new town was changed to Huntsville in honor of the first settler, John Hunt.

LeRoy Pope House ca. 1930

Huntsville is the county seat of Madison County and its population in the 2010 census was 180,105.

Mooresville, Limestone County, Alabama

Even though it encompasses only sixty-four acres, Mooresville claims to be the oldest incorporated town in the new Alabama Territory. It was incorporated on November 16, 1818 and has a connection with two Presidents of the United States. The town has the oldest, still operational post office in the state of Alabama.

Mooresville is the site of Old House, in which President Andrew Johnson, the 17th President of the United States, was a tailor for a short time. President James A. Garfield preached in Mooresville in the old white clapboard Church of Christ in 1862, while he was encamped nearby during the Civil War.

Located twenty miles southwest of Huntsville in Limestone County, Mooresville is the first incorporated town in the Alabama Territory.

Some of present day trees in Mooresville may date back to the 1800's.

Mooresville Post Office 1934 (Library of Congress)

Prior to the settlers, the Chickasaws resided in the area of Mooresville. In 1818, Mooresville had sixty-two residents and petitioned the Territorial Legislature for an Act of Incorporation, a year earlier than when Alabama became a state.

Today, the entire town, characterized as a picturesque early 19th century village, is listed on the National Register of Historic Places. The town was the primary filming location for Disney's *Tom and Huck.*

The population of the town was fifty-nine according to the 2000 census.

Claiborne, Monroe County, Alabama

Claiborne is a ghost town on a bluff high above the Alabama River in Monroe County, Alabama, but in the early 1800s, it was a busy place.

Following the Revolutionary war Claiborne became one of the largest and fastest growing communities in what would become

Alabama. Early settlers included three future Alabama governors: John Gayle, John Murphy, and Arthur P. Bagby. William B. Travis, a hero of the Alamo, lived in Claiborne for many years before leaving for Texas in 1831. Other prominent politicians included James Dellet and Charles Tait." James Dellet's house is the only original residence remaining in Claiborne.

Claiborne Masonic Lodge ca. 1934 (Library of Congress)

Marquis de Lafayette visited Claiborne in April 1825 during his famous tour of all twenty-four American States. He was entertained in the newly built masonic hall, a building which, along with the William B. Travis house, still exists but was later moved to the nearby community of Perdue Hill.

Outbreaks of yellow fever and cholera stemmed growth and after the Civil War, the town quickly lost importance in the new economy. By 2008 the site contained only the James Dellet House and three 19th century cemeteries.

Fort Claiborne is situated at the head of schooner navigation on the Alabama River, about 130 miles from Blakely by water, and one hundred and eighty by land.

Blakely, Baldwin County, Alabama

During the height of its existence, Blakeley was a thriving town which flourished as a competitor to its western neighbor, Mobile. The town is now in an Alabama historic state park known as Historic Blakeley State Park near Spanish Fort.

Native Americans lived in the area prior to European settlers arriving. Blakeley was founded by Josiah Blakeley "an entrepreneur and adventurer from Connecticut who moved to Mobile in 1806." He bought 7,000 acres of land in the northeastern portion of Mobile Bay at the old seat of the Apalaches, where the Bayor Salome empties into the Tensaw.

Blakeley lived on the Polecat Bay side of his island, above Coffee Bayou, just across the river from Mobile. When he bought from Joseph Collins, the surveyor in 1807, there was already an unfinished dwelling on it, with a well-ditched plantation growing rice, corn, cotton, domestic grasses, and vegetables.

Joseph Collins appears to have been its first owner, having acquired it by permit of Osorno April 26, 1803. No Spanish survey seems to have been made, and so later its acreages was found to be 2280, instead of the estimated 4000. He sold it in 1807 to Josiah Blakeley, of Connecticut, for $1500. In the deed Collins describes it as seven miles long. This Yankee made it a plantation, which he called Festino.

The oath of allegiance of Josiah Blakeley to the Spanish Crown exists in the archives at Mobile, bearing the date July 10, 1810, The paper recites that he had already lived four years in the district, and had since 1807 cultivated an island purchased from Don Jose Collins.

On January 6, 1814, the Mississippi Territorial Legislature authorized him to lay out a town to be known as Blakeley.

Josiah Blakeley died in 1815 and did not live to see the admission of Alabama to Statehood in 1819.

Old Cahawba, Dallas County, Alabama

Cahaba (also spelled Cahawba) was the first State Capital of Alabama.

Old Cahaba State Marker ca. 1934 (Library of Congress)

By an act of the legislature, passed February 13, 1818, Clement C. Clay, Samuel Taylor, Samuel Dale, James Titus, and William. L. Adams were appointed commissioners to select the most central and eligible location for the seat of government of the newly established Alabama Territory.

The commissioners, after investigation, reported a site at the mouth of the Cahaba River, in the recently formed county of Dallas, as the most suitable location. Their report was concurred in, and an act was passed November 21, 1818, fixing this locality the permanent capital.

The governor was named as commissioner to lay off the town into lots, and to sell them at public sale. By an act of December 13, 1819, Cahaba was fixed on as the seat of justice of Dallas County. The place was, therefore, at the same time the capital of the State and the seat of justice of Dallas County. It became at once a thriving business and an attractive social center.

The original choice of Cahaba had not long been made before it became apparent that the place had many disadvantages as a town site. Its situation was low, subjecting it to over-flow from both rivers, so that at times it was almost impossible to reach the statehouse without a conveyance by water.

In 1825 came the largest flood on record in the history of the state. The almost complete inundation of the town hastened the decision of the legislature to choose a new location. Tuscaloosa was selected, and the public offices, property and records were removed.

In consequence of the flood and the removal of the capitol, many influential citizens left the town, and for a time it dwindled into an insignificant village. But in a few years it began to revive, and by the early thirties it was again a populous town, and the most important shipping point on the Alabama River.

Large warehouses and stores were built, old residences repaired, new ones of excellent architectural design erected, and with the coming of many wealthy families, and an unusual number of men eminent in statesmanship, law and medical science, these combined, gave Cahaba an air of prosperity to which no other Alabama town could at that early period furnish a parallel.

Many men prominent in Alabama and national History resided in Cahaba. Of these may be mentioned Horatio G. Perry, George W. Gayle, Jesse Beene, George R. Evans, Lawrence E. Dawson, William L. Yancey, Col. C. C. Pegues, John S. Hunter, P. J. Wood, Gen. John T. Morgan, Judge B. F. Saffold, Daniel S. Troy, Gen. E. W. Pettus, Col. H. R. Dawson, Dr. E. G. Ulmer, Dr. Thomas Casey, Dr. Jabez Heutis, Joel E. Matthews, Charles Matthews, both millionaire planters, Robert S. Hatcher, Edward M. Perrine and Samuel M. Hill, both merchant princes. Cahaba was in the zenith of its prosperity at the outbreak of the War in 1861.

Colonel Rees D. Gayle house ca. 1934 (Library of Congress)

In the early part of March, 1865, the place was visited by another disastrous flood. After the waters had subsided, the Federal prisoners were all paroled and sent to Vicksburg, and the post at Cahaba was abandoned.

The flood, followed soon after by the close of the War, and by the freedom of the slaves, involving the utter demoralization of labor, brought about the rapid decline of Cahaba. The end came in 1866 when the court house was removed to Selma, under an act of December 14, 1865. Many of the citizens of Cahaba removed also. Others moved to distant localities, and a few years later Cahaba,

112

once one of the most noted towns of central Alabama, was left empty and desolate.

Selma, Dallas County, Alabama

Selma is one of the oldest surviving cities in Alabama. Located on a high bluff of the north bank of the Alabama River in Dallas County, Selma is near the geographical center of the State.

St. James Hotel, Selma, Alabama 1939

Thomas Moore was the first white settler in the vicinity of what would later become Selma. In 1816, Thomas Moore settled in what was originally known as High Soap Stone Bluff. After Thomas Moore built his log cabin, the area was renamed Moore's Bluff. In 1817, John Simpson built a log house where James J. Bryan's store later located followed by a log house built by Elias Parkman. A large log house was built at the corner of where Greene and Water street by Mike Woodall for an eating house, or hotel. It was in this house that General LaFayette was entertained in 1825.

Colonel William Rufus King, who later became Vice-President of the

United States, located three miles south of Selma around 1818, and took an active part in establishing the town of Selma.

Colonel King was a young diplomat, first in Naples and later to St. Petersburg, Russia, prior to his move to Alabama. After completing his Russian tenure, he followed his older brother brother, Thomas DeVane King to Alabama. His brother settled in Tuscaloosa, Alabama, while Colonel W. R. King settled on a large bend on the Alabama River in Dallas County. There he built his home, *Chestnut Hill.*

On the 16th and 18th of March, 1819, before Alabama was admitted as a State into the Union, William Rufus King and George Phillips bought from the United States all of section 36, township 17, range 10, and section 31, township 17, range 11, lying north of the river, which equaled about 1,101 acres.

A company was organized for the purpose of laying these lands off into a town.

Colonel William Rufus King, upon perfecting the organization of the company, was given the privilege of naming the town. Being of a literary turn of mind, and fond of the writings of ancient poets, he named the new town Selma. The name comes from Ossian's epic poems *Songs of Selma.* Ossian, a blind poet, was the narrator and purported author of a cycle of epic poems published by the Scottish poet James Macpherson around 1760.

The city of Selma in Dallas County, Alabama is now known world-wide due to its prominence in the Civil Rights struggles and march from the Edmund Pettus bridge to Montgomery, Alabama.

Native Americans Deceived By British

British agents continued to acquaint the Indians with the hostile attitude of England with the United States, and told them that war would soon come. Then the British would swoop down on the country and capture it so the Creeks sided with the English.

A story is told that once a cunning chief, Oce-Oche-Motla, from the falls of the Black Warrior was annually given credit by Mr. Gaines to the amount of a hundred dollars. When he heard the news of the English coming, Oce-Oche-Motla tried to get credit for a thousand dollars. He believed that no one would be at the trading-house to receive payment when it fell due.

Oce-oche-Motla offered his staunch friend, Tandy Walker as security for so large a credit. Mr. Gaines mentioned his troubles with the English and refused the increased credit. The chief insisted so Mr. Gaines told him they should sleep over the matter and let each tell his dream in the morning.

Tandy Walker secretly met Mr. Gaines at midnight at 'the Rock,' overhanging the river's bluff and told the treachery of the chief and the preparations for the Creek War.

The next morning Mr. Gaines related his dream to be that the United States and the English would fight, the English would be whipped, and the northern tribes siding with the English would suffer and that he must not give the large credit. He gave the chief the accustomed hundred-dollar credit, and never afterward saw him again.

BIBLIOGRAPHY

1. Bancroft's *History of the United States*

2. Ball, Rev. T. H. *The Great Southeast or Clarke County and its Surroundings,* pub. 1882

3. Brewer, Willis *Alabama, Her History, Resource, War Record and Public Men: from 1540 to 1872*, 1872

4. Du Bose, Joel Campbell *Sketches of Alabama History*, 1901

5. Pickett, Albert James *History of Alabama and incidentally of Mississpipi and Georgia,* 1896; Mississippi Dept. of Archives

6. Hamilton, *Mobile of the five flags* (1913), pp. 130, 190, 211;

7. Hamilton, *Colonial Mobile* (1910), pp. 217, 252, 255, 266, 309, 412, 478.

8. Saunders, Col James Edmonds *Early Settlers of Alabama Notes and Genealogies, 1899*

9. Knight Jr. VJ, editor. *The Search for Mabila: The Decisive Battle between Hernando de Soto and Chief Tascalusa.* Tuscaloosa: University of Alabama Press, 2009

10. Hooper, J. J, editor, *Woodward's Reminiscenses; A Personal Account of the Creek Nation in Georgia and Alabama,* by General Thomas S. Woodward, Published: Montgomery, Ala.; Barrett & Wimbish, Book and General Job Printers, 1859

Additional information on Alabama can be found on the websites:

www.alabamapioneers.com

www.daysgoneby.me

Follow on Facebook at:

http://www.facebook.com/alabamapioneers

http://www.facebook.com/daysgonebyme

and

Twitter

http://twitter.com/alabamapioneers

Other nonfiction and fictional books by Donna R. Causey can be found
at
Barnes and Noble
or
Amazon.com

Follow Donna R. Causey on

www.facebook.com/alabamapioneers

www.facebook.com/daysgonebyme

http://www.facebook.com/ribbonoflove

or on

Donna R. Causey's websites

www.alabamapioneers.com

www.daysgoneby.me

Made in the USA
San Bernardino, CA
23 December 2015